Seacoast Scituate

By Air

Lyle Nyberg, Gary Banks, Bill Richardson

Published by Lyle Nyberg, www.lylenyberg.com
Scituate, Massachusetts, 2022

ISBN: 978-1-7354745-6-4 (paperback)

Cover: Design by Susannah Green using (1) aerial photos of Scituate harbor and seacoast by Gary M. Banks, William E. Richardson, and (2) photo of authors by Jean A. Richardson 2022.

Inside: Aerial photos by Gary M. Banks, William E. Richardson (except as noted); town seal and maps in public domain.

Contents

Introduction 1

1 The Glades, Bassing Beach, Gulph, North Scituate 5

2 Minot, Mann Hill, Shore Acres, Sand Hills..15

3 Scituate Harbor, Cedar Point, First Cliff 21

4 Second Cliff, Peggotty Beach..27

5 Third Cliff, The Driftway...33

6 North River, The Spit..39

7 Fourth Cliff, Humarock, South River 45

Notes...49

About the Authors 51

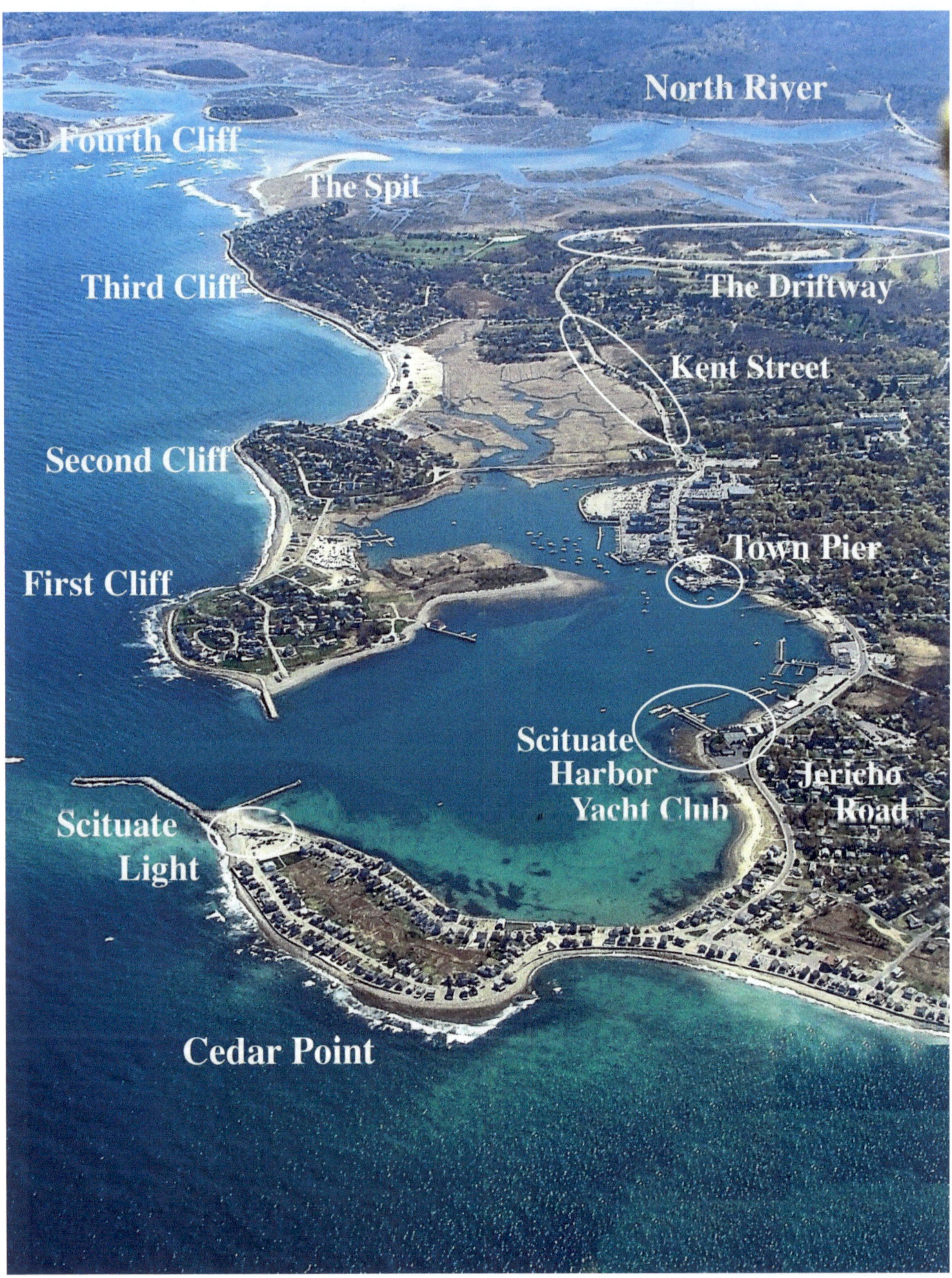

The cover shows Scituate Harbor looking south, with Massachusetts Bay at left. Town roads (the Driftway, Kent Street, Front Street, Jericho Road) run down the shore to Cedar Point. At point's end is Old Scituate Light (1811), looking small from this height. Here, the main part of the harbor has a heart shape. This book has other seacoast sights, including Bassing Beach, the Glades, and North Scituate Beach. [1/1/03]

Introduction

We can all use a different perspective on things at times. Let's take to the air and get a fresh look at the scenic area around us.

This book highlights the diverse landscape of the seacoast along a South Shore town. Scituate, Massachusetts, is midway between Boston and Plymouth. It has a most picturesque and varied seacoast, with harbors, rivers, islands, and beaches. It is noted for its four cliffs facing the ocean. The coast is rocky, particularly in the north, and sandy further south.

Scituate (also called Satuit in times past) is an old town with a name taken from the Native American word for the cold brook that runs into the harbor.

Scituate's historic coastline — at least 10 miles long — has been well documented. It has been charted over centuries, including on Capt. John Smith's early 1600s map of New England. The town's name appears (as "Siticate") on a map of 1634, not long before Scituate's incorporation as a town in 1636. Scituate's coastline appears on a 1776 map prepared for the British Navy during the American rebellion. In addition, a 1903 atlas records the town's coastline, along with its houses and their owners.[1]

The first known aerial photograph was taken in 1858 from a balloon in Paris by the Frenchman "Nadar." The oldest surviving aerial photo was takin in 1860 from a balloon in Boston by James Wallace Black.[2]

With the development of the airplane, there have been many aerial photos of Scituate's seacoast. Some were taken as early as 1937. Others appear on vintage postcards, such as "Cliff Hotel from the air, North Scituate Beach, Mass." published by the well-known Tichnor Brothers company in Boston. (The Tichnors, by the way, had roots in Scituate.)[3]

Often, the aerial photos were commercial, sold door-to-door by the individual pilot/photographer who took them. Exceptional examples are displayed at the Mill Wharf Restaurant in Scituate Harbor.

Later came comprehensive aerial surveys of the town, commissioned by the town. The Town Archives has two sets of note. First is a bound set of 30–40 large printed photos in black and white, taken about 1954–1961. Second is a comprehensive set of hundreds of aerial photos, taken for the town in 1968. They are black and white interpositives, like enormous negatives. In addition, various consultants' reports to the town contain aerial photos.

Drones now provide great photos of the town's coastline. Usually these are commissioned to promote the sale of a particular real estate property. More general examples exist. Karl Swenson's spectacular photo of winter storm Riley's flooding at Peggotty Beach appeared as a two-page spread in TIME magazine's March 2018 issue.[4]

Satellite imaging has produced services like Google Maps and Google Earth. We can now conveniently view digital photos and maps of Scituate's coastline. Since these are updated from time to time, they may not retain past images. In addition, they may not be convenient for everyone, or provide a desired angle, focus, or resolution.

This book presents a curated set of splendid photos of Scituate's scenic seacoast by air. They are in color, in a handy form. We believe this is the first such book of its kind. You might think of it as a picture companion to other books about the history of Scituate's cliffs and seacoast.[5]

Some of the amazing residents of Scituate created this book with their experience in aviation, photography, book design, cover design, and history. We hope you enjoy these views!

Lyle Nyberg
Third Cliff, Scituate, Massachusetts
March 2022

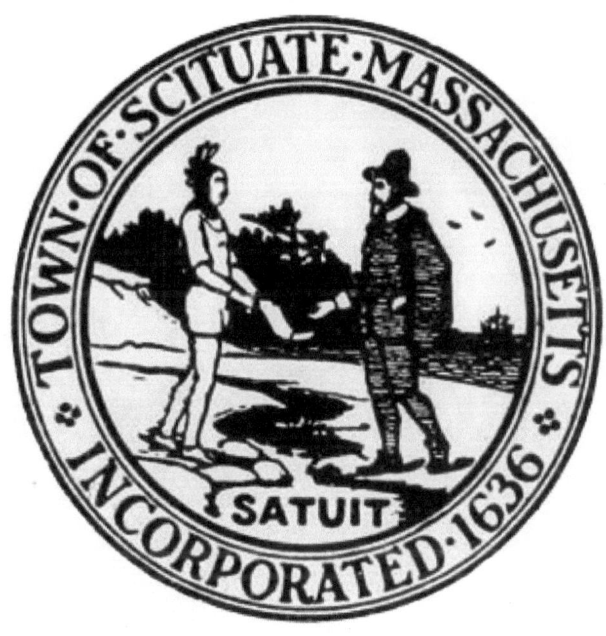

Town seal, showing cliff, Satuit Brook, Native American, English settler, and ship on ocean

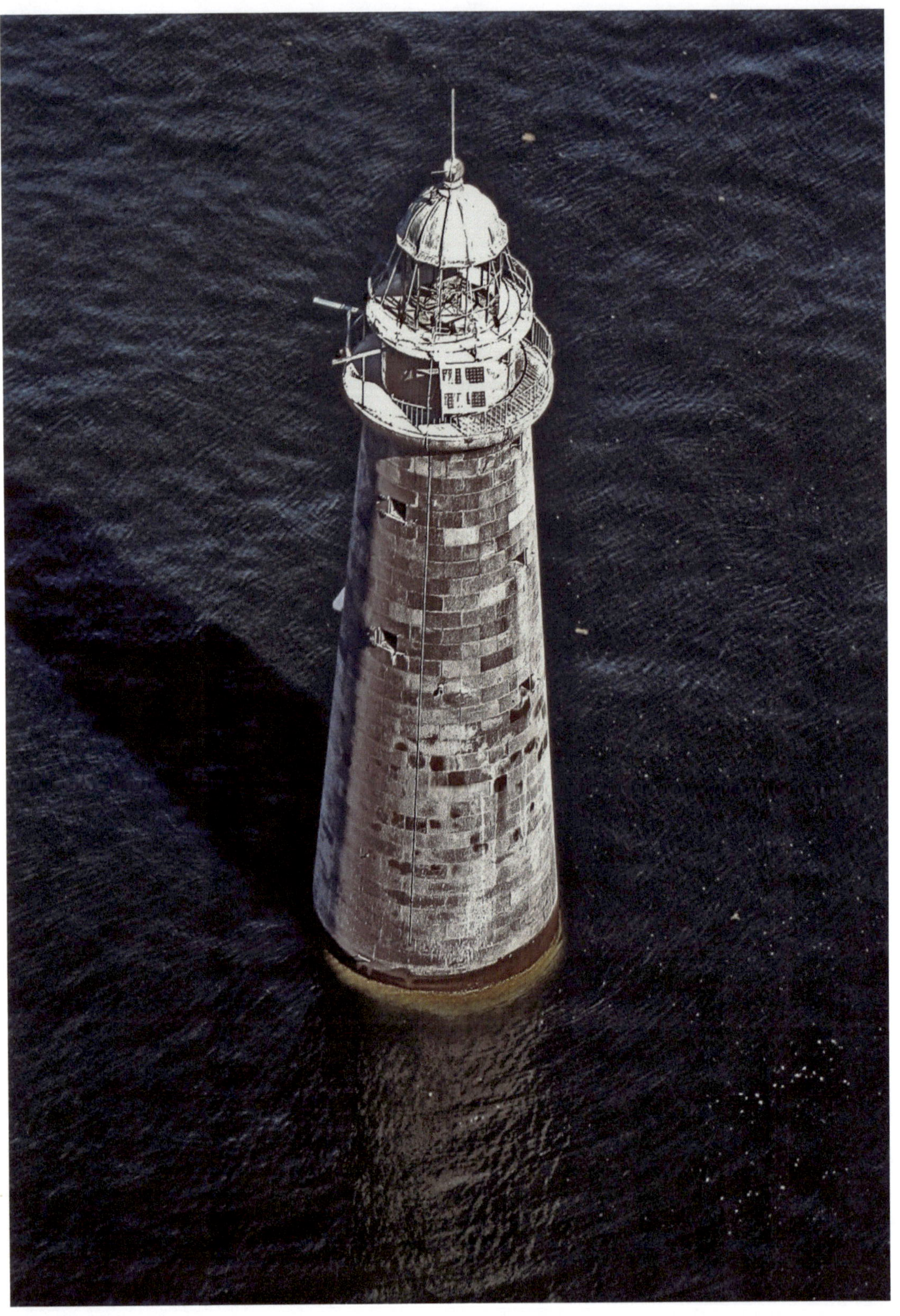

1 Minot's Ledge Light (1860). Lighthouse over a mile offshore of northern Scituate that flashes 1-4-3, "I love you" from light installed in 1894. [9/15/16]

1

THE GLADES, BASSING BEACH, GULPH, NORTH SCITUATE

The north of Scituate is scenic, complex, and historic. It has attracted summer visitors since the 1800s, including Henry David Thoreau.

Its rocky coast presents risks to ships. As an aid to navigation, Minot Light (Minot's Ledge Light) was completed in 1850. It was destroyed in an 1851 storm that took the lives of its two keepers. The current tower, built with 1,079 blocks of Quincy granite, dates from 1860. In 2014, it was sold to philanthropist Bobby Sager. It is extensively documented, and is often pictured with stormy waves splashing as high as the light.[6]

The rocky northern point of Scituate is Strawberry Point, better known as the Glades. A former hotel building, built in 1846, still stands there, making it one of the oldest remaining American hotel buildings. In the 1870s, the area was acquired by the Glades Association, with members that included the presidential Adams family. It remains a private enclave used mostly in the summer.[7]

Bassing Beach, an island, is part of Scituate, even though it defines one side of Cohasset Harbor, and the Cohasset Conservation Trust owns more than 12 acres of the island. It is accessible by boat, home to two remaining cottages out of the original 20 when the beach was used for drying fish, making ropes (a ropewalk), gunning for ducks, and fishing for bass, or "bassing," thus its name.[8]

The Gulph River empties into Cohasset Harbor. It is fed by Musquashcut Brook, "the Gulf" brook, and Bound Brook. A bridge crosses Bound Brook on Mordecai Lincoln Road, just off Country Way. Here is a mill owned in the late 1600s by an ancestor of Abraham Lincoln. Scituate's town meeting in 2020 authorized the purchase of the Mordecai Lincoln property in North Scituate for historic preservation.[9]

North Scituate Beach is both a beach and a premier summer colony established in the late 1800s. In 1899, the Hatherly Country Club was founded here. North Scituate Beach also was the location of the Cliff Hotel and a summer home of Boston mayor James Michael Curley.[10]

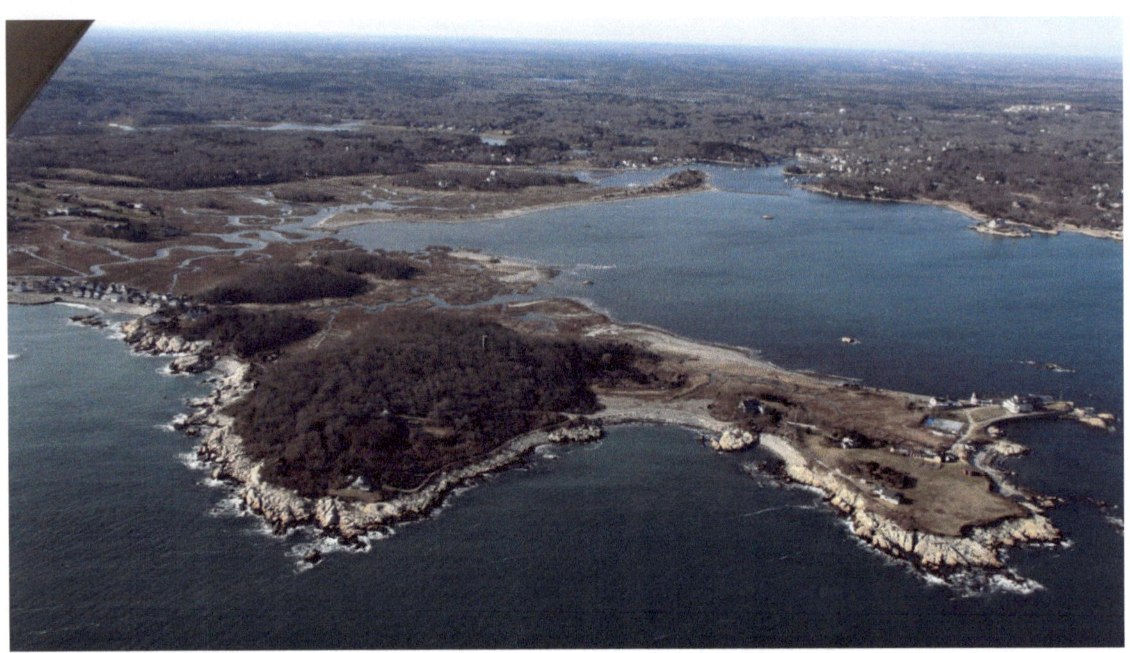

2 Panorama of the Glades coastline, looking west, with Bassing Beach (center) leading to Cohasset Harbor. At left, part of Minot Beach. [2/3/12]

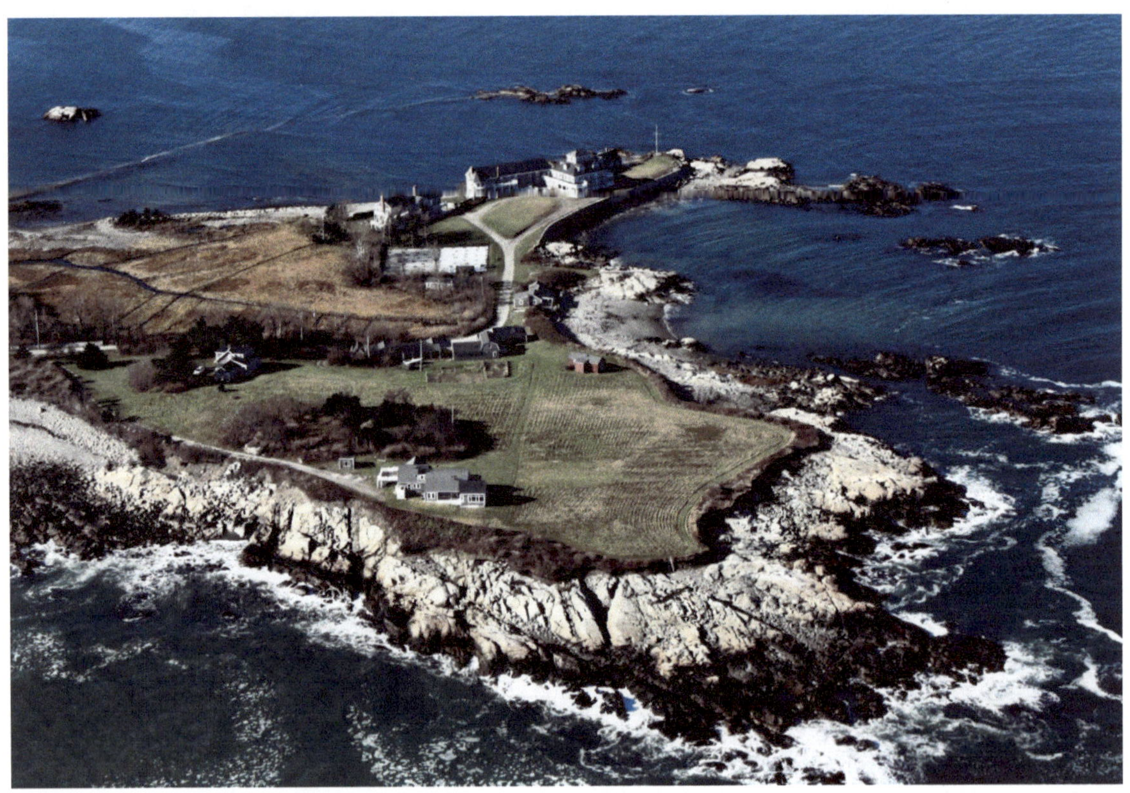

3 View of the Glades (Strawberry Point). Large building top center was once a hotel. Directly below it, the small red building in the center was a lifesaving station of the Humane Society of Massachusetts. [11/12/21]

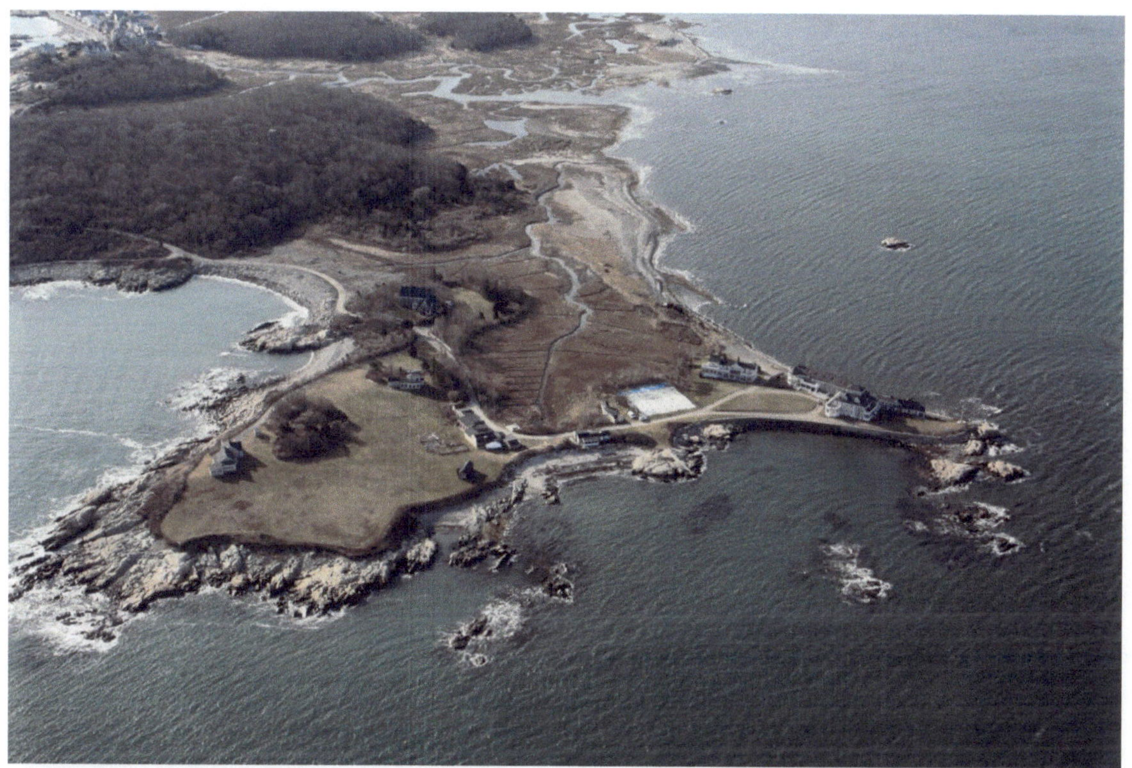

4 Another view of the Glades, looking south, showing Strawberry Point's rugged granite ledges, formed 350 million years ago when linked to the Irish and Moroccan coasts. [2/3/12]

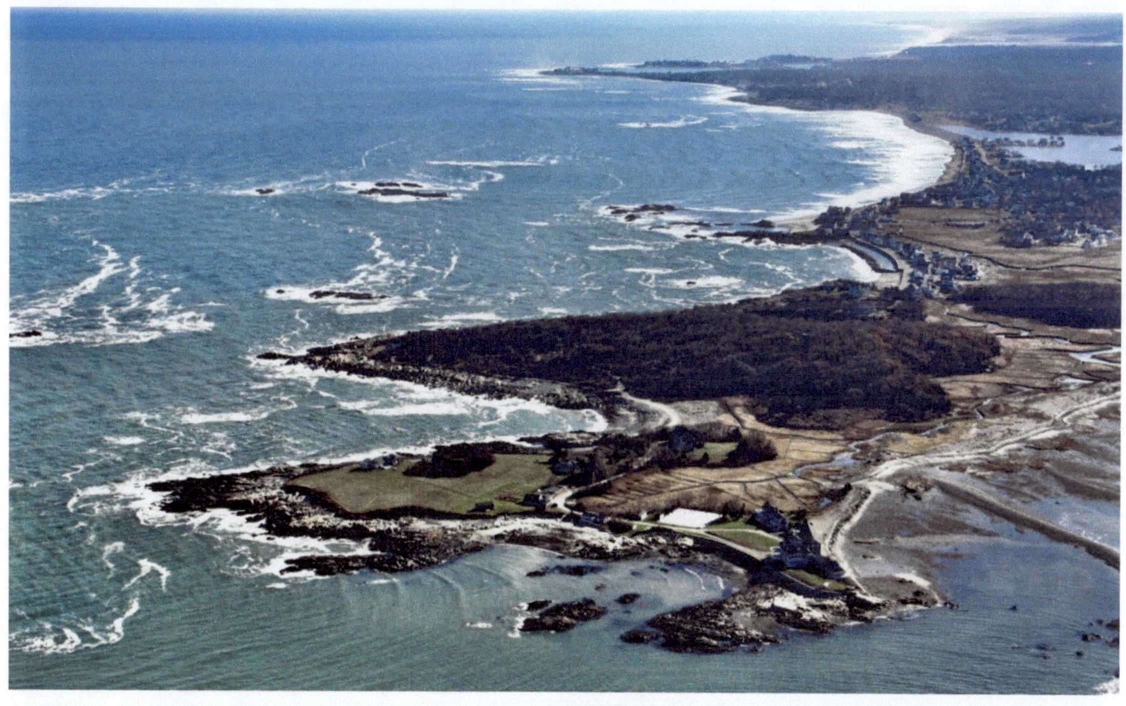

5 View of the entire seacoast of Scituate, looking south, with the Glades in the foreground, then Minot, North Scituate Beach, Scituate Harbor, and the Cliffs. At upper right is Musquashcut Pond. [11/21/19]

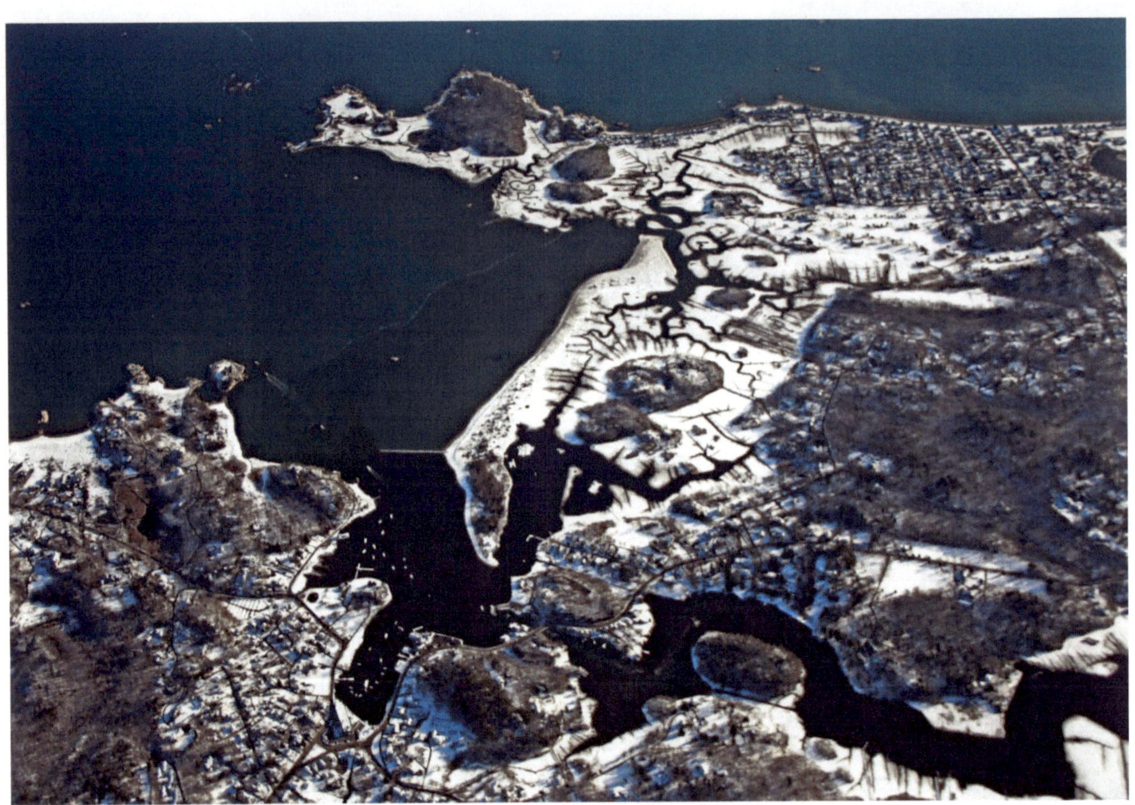

6 View looking east. At top, the Glades, Minot, North Scituate Beach. At bottom, Gulph River emptying into Cohasset Harbor, Cohasset Cove. At center, Bassing Beach, with Briggs Harbor at top center. [2/6/16]

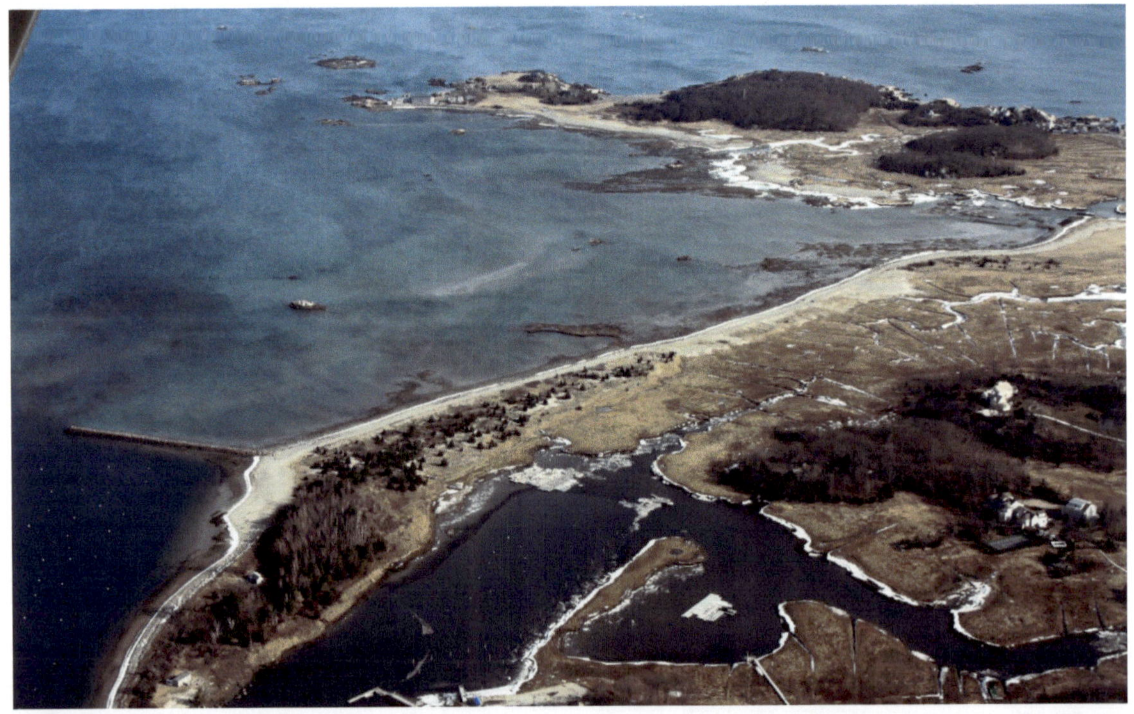

7 Bassing Beach, with two cottages at bottom left. At top, the Glades. [1/26/18]

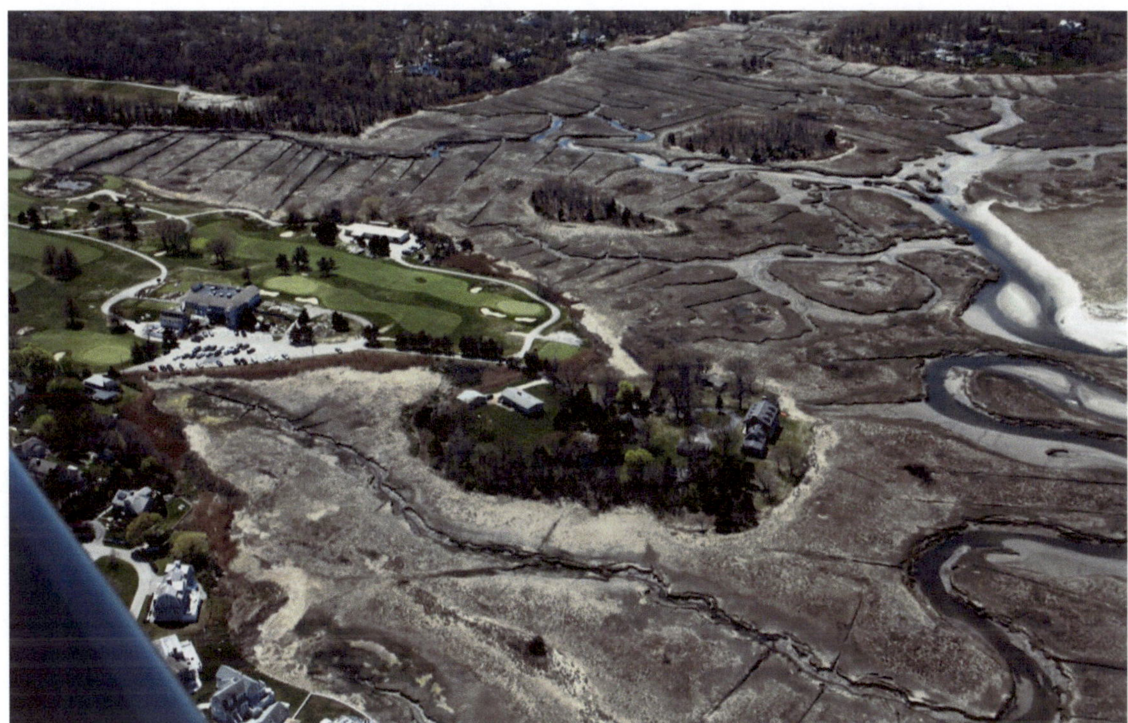

8 View looking west of Hatherly Country Club golf course (center left), with Treasure Island to its right, in center, with two houses visible. Beyond the club is an unnamed island (Fane?), Horse Island, Wood Island, and Bailey's Island (upper right). Latter two islands have houses. Bassing Beach is to the right. [5/14/20]

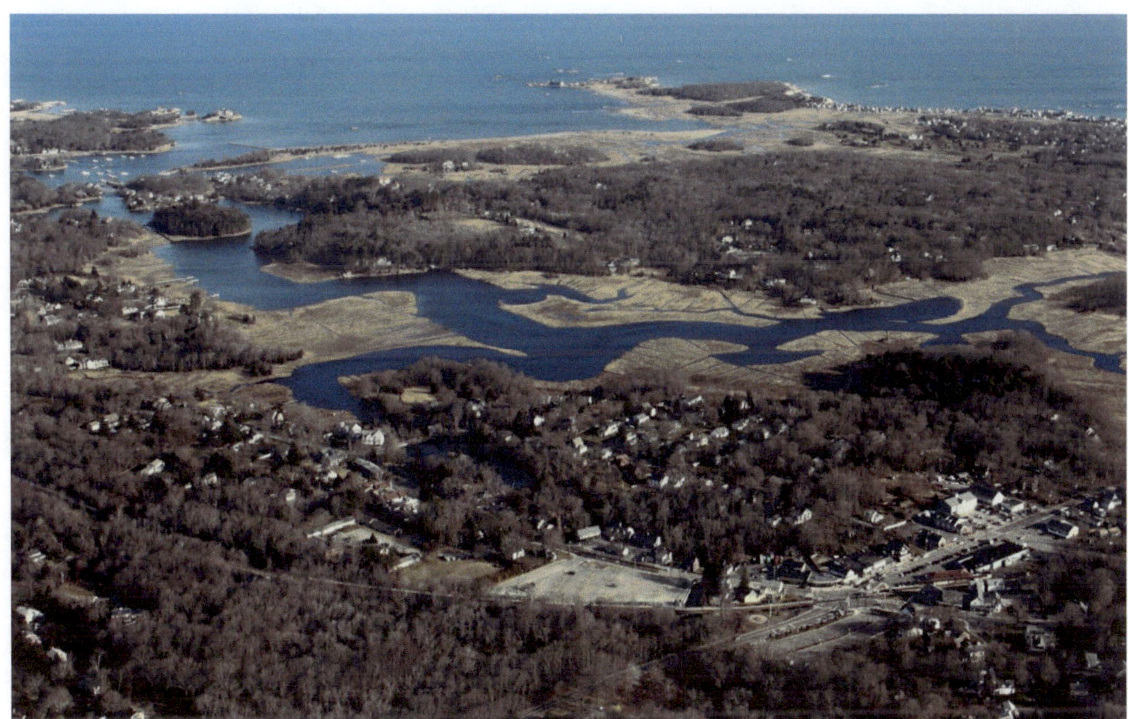

9 View looking northeast. From top: the Glades; Bassing Beach and nearby islands; Musquashcut Brook (far right, center, upper) and The Gulf (far right, center, lower) feeding the Gulph River, entering Cohasset Harbor; North Scituate intersection of Country Way, Gannett Road, and commuter rail line with parking lot. [2/3/12]

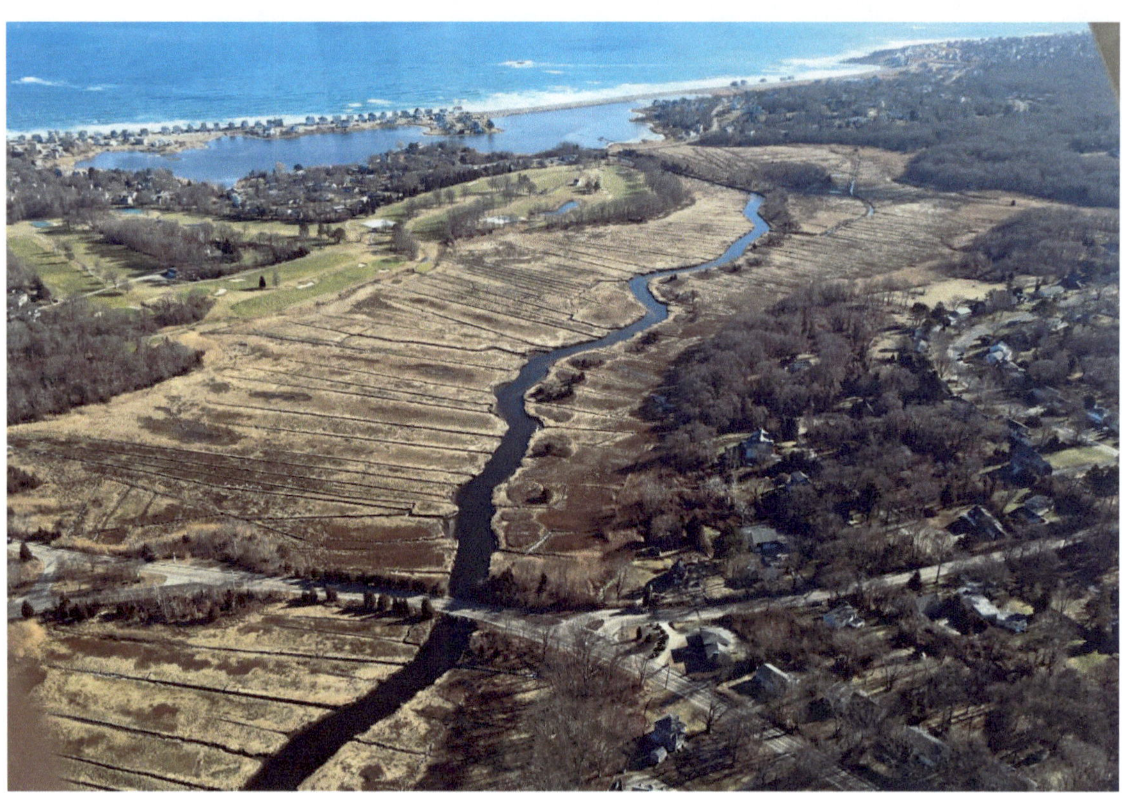

10 View looking south. North Scituate Beach at upper left, Musquashcut Pond and shore at top, Musquashcut Brook leading from pond at center. Gannett Road - Hollett Street intersection at center foreground. [n.d.]

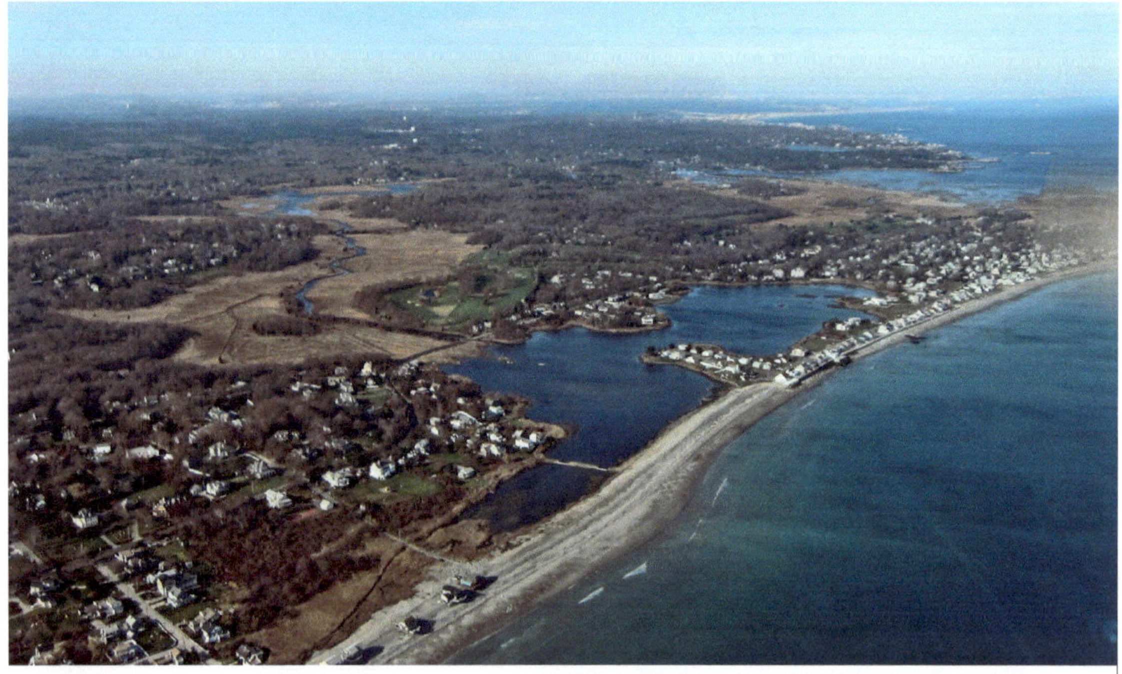

11 View looking north. From bottom, Mann Hill Beach, Musquashcut Pond, North Scituate Beach. The pond, separated only by a narrow rocky barrier beach from the ocean, turns away and drains into the Gulf which makes up the Gulph River, flowing into Cohasset Harbor, emptying into the ocean miles north. [n.d.]

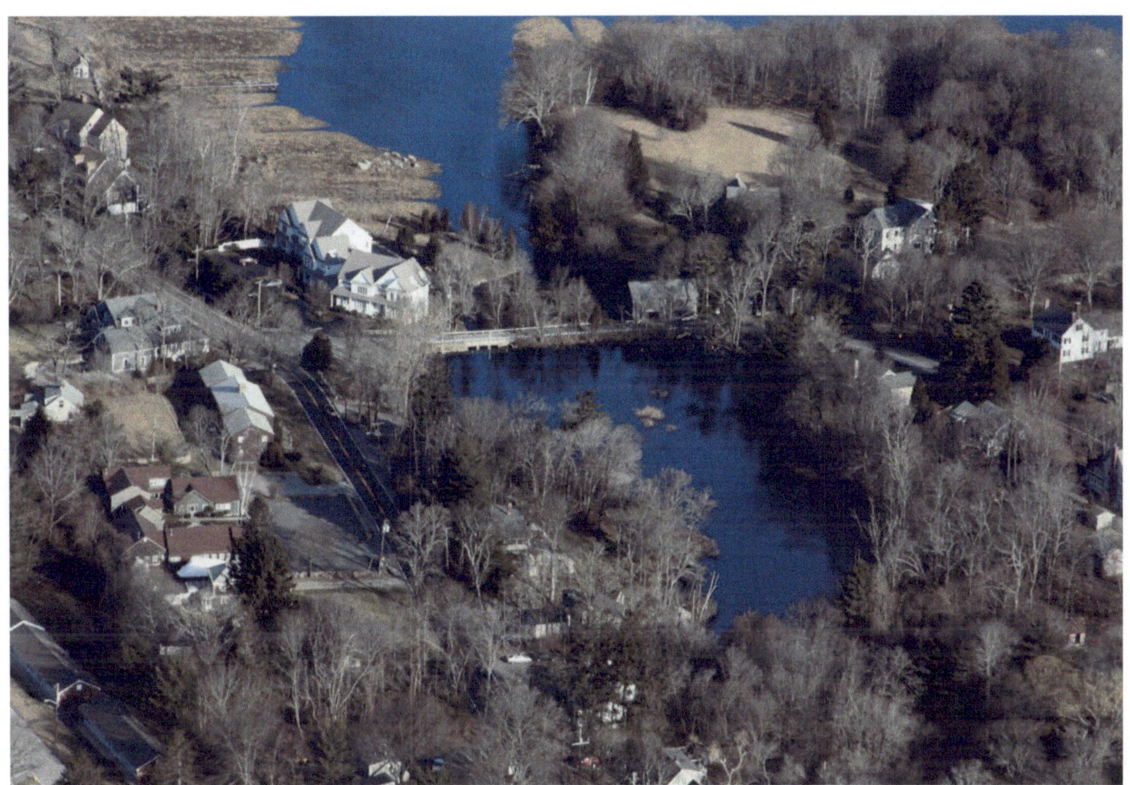

12 In North Scituate, Mordecai Lincoln Road runs from near Country Way across Bound Brook and then-existing Hunters Pond, site of mill owned by ancestor of Pres. Abraham Lincoln in 1690s. [2/3/12]

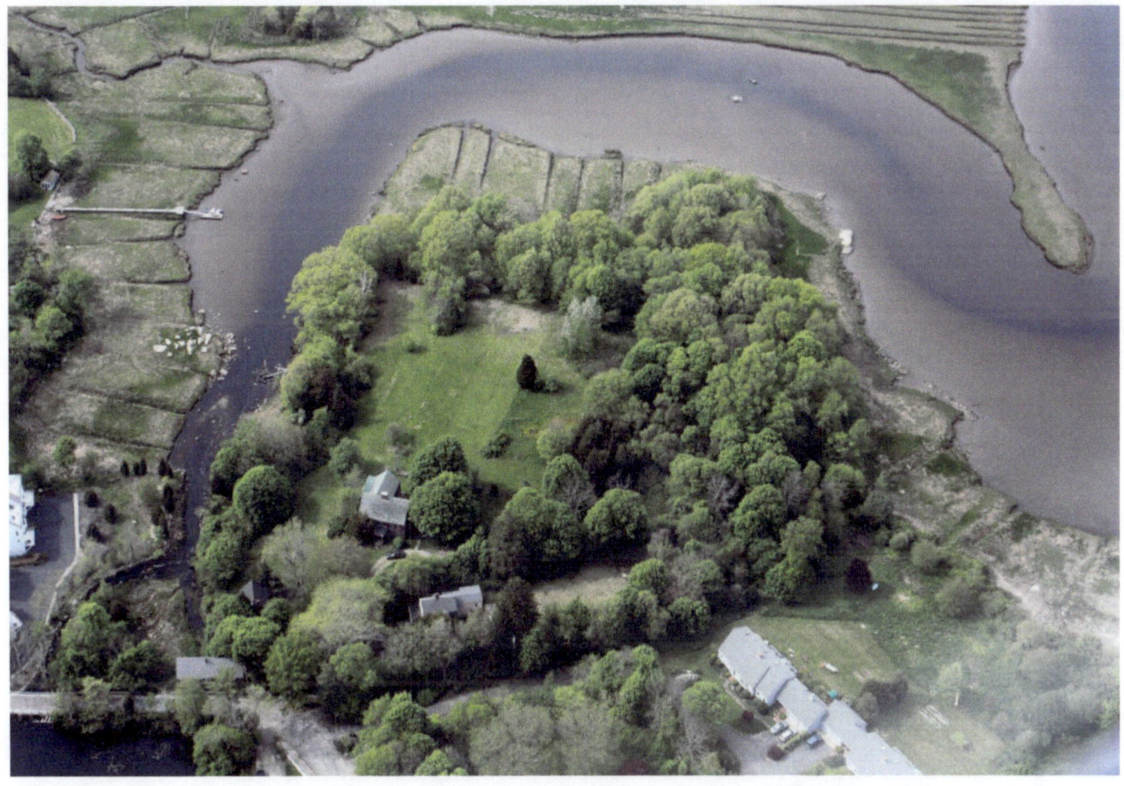

13 Another view of Mordecai Lincoln property, which Scituate Town Meeting voted to purchase. [5/20/09]

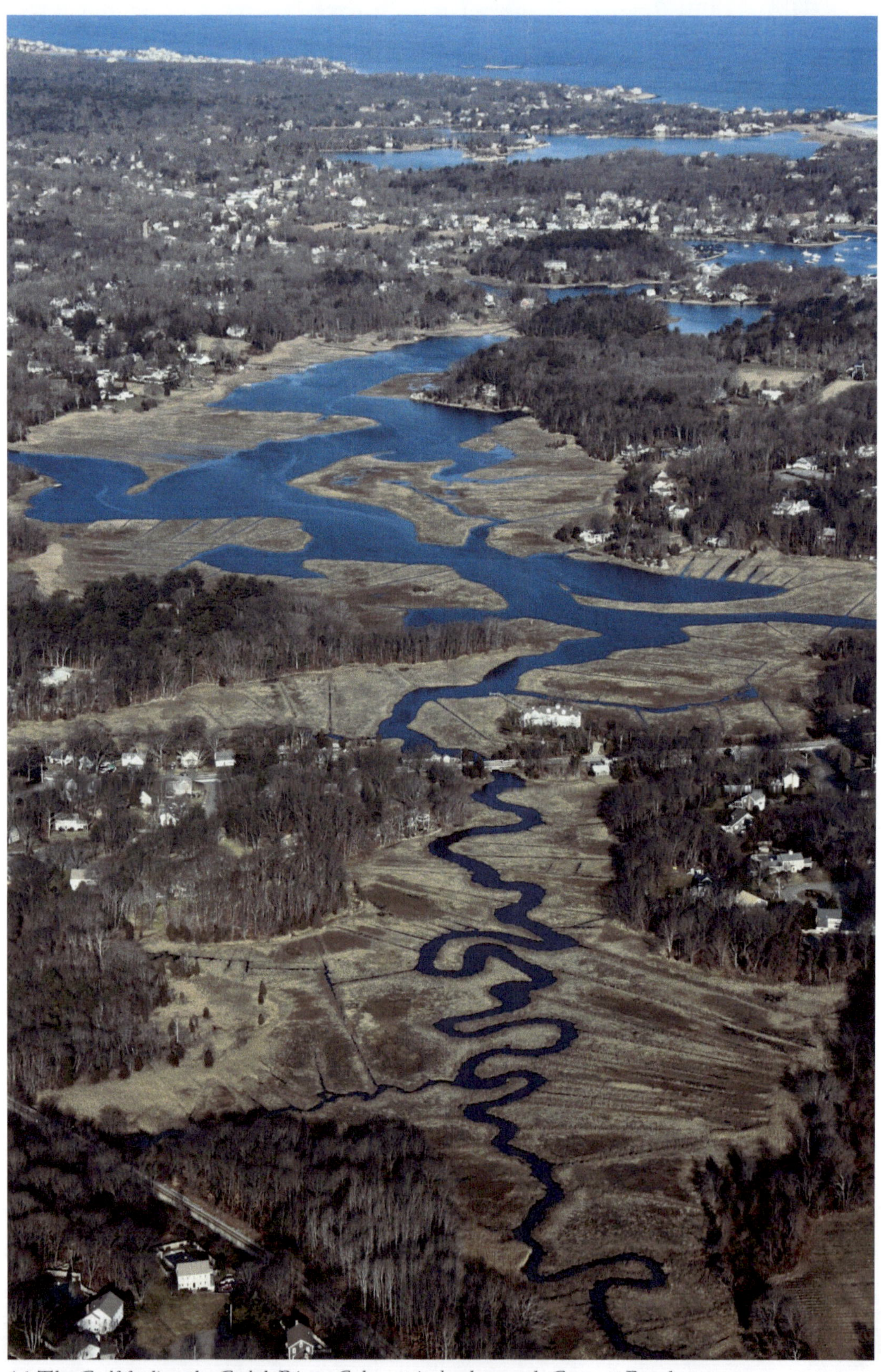

14 The Gulf feeding the Gulph River, Cohasset in background. Gannett Road across center. [2/3/12]

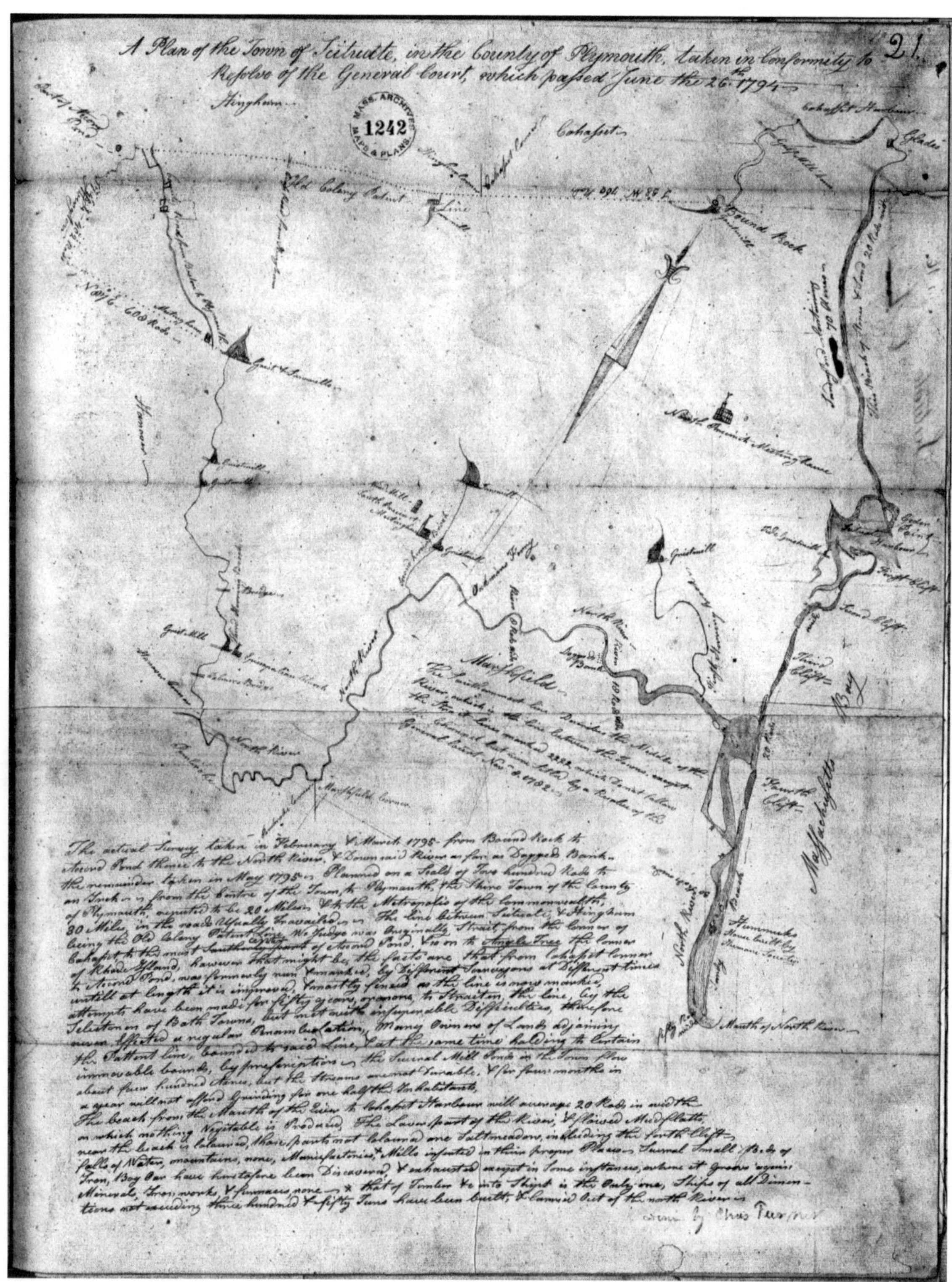

15 Turner 1795 map. Looking north half way up the page on the right is Scituate Harbor. Labels for First through Fourth "Clifts" and "Hummocks." Courtesy of Massachusetts State Archives.

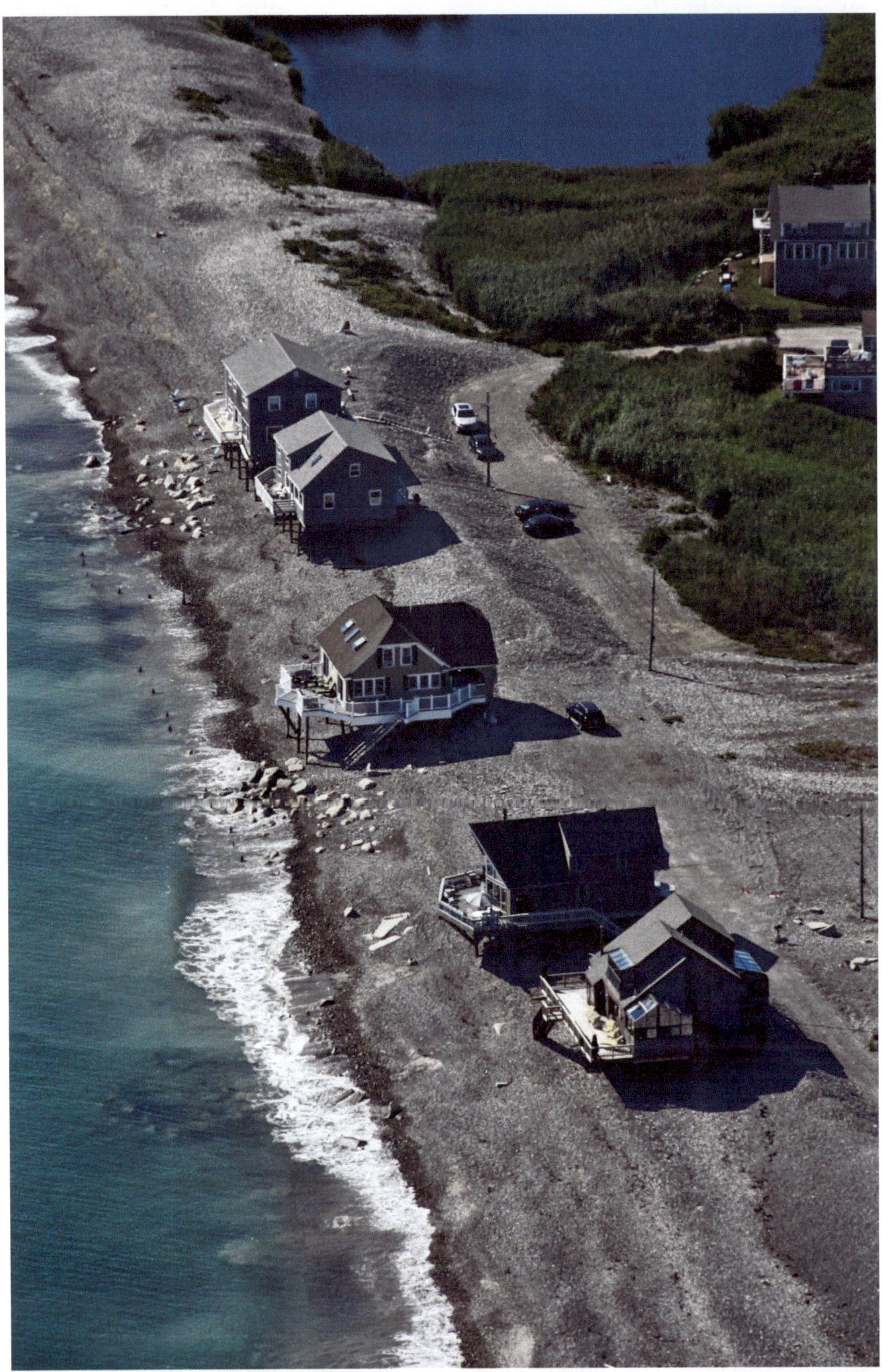

1 Ocean-front beach cottages, end of Mann Hill Road. [7/15/16]

2

MINOT, MANN HILL, SHORE ACRES, SAND HILLS

Scituate's coast has many beaches. Moving south from the Glades, we find Minot Beach, North Scituate Beach (see previous chapter), Mann Hill Beach, Egypt Beach, Shore Acres, and Sand Hills. Here are summer cottages galore. Many of these have become year-round residences.

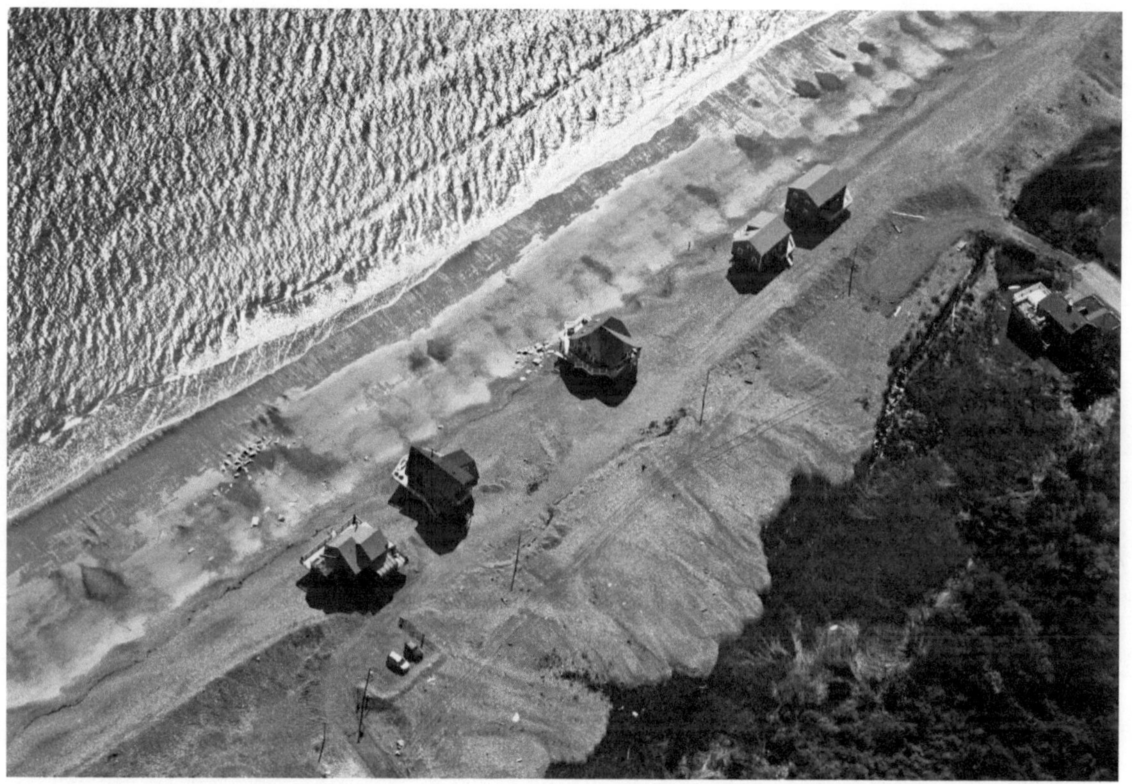

2 Same five cottages at Mann Hill Beach. Note the overflowing of the beach onto the marsh. [5/10/19]

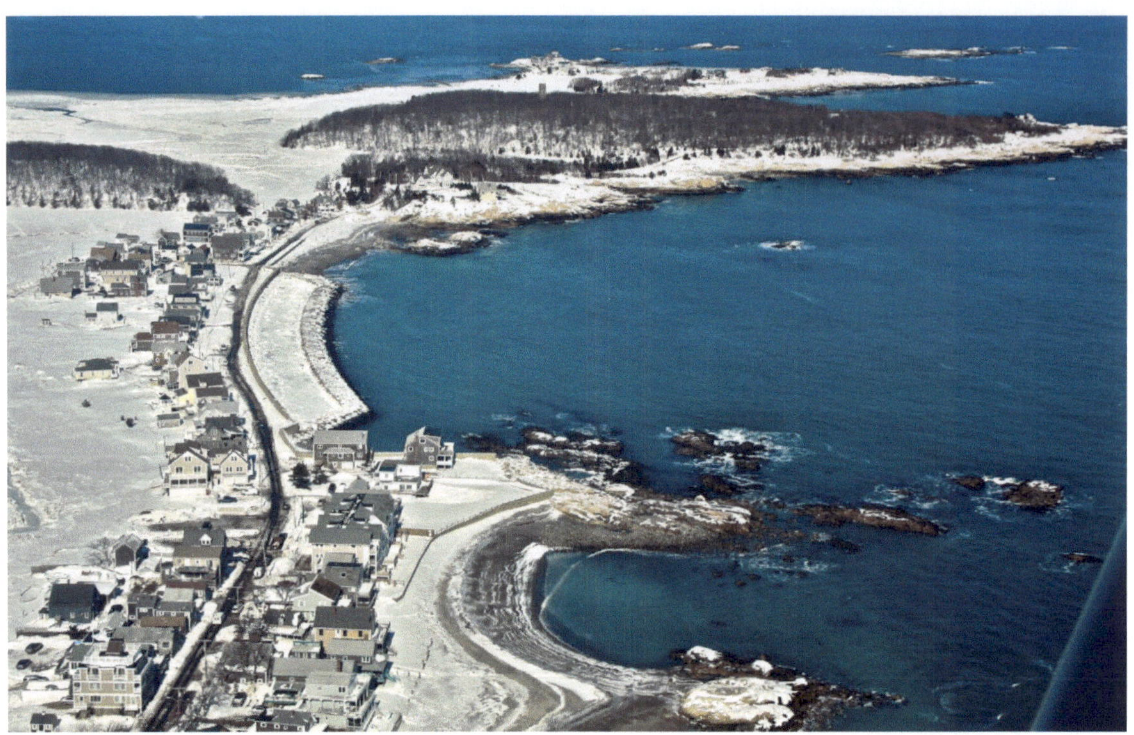

3 Minot Beach in winter, with the Glades in background. [2/27/15]

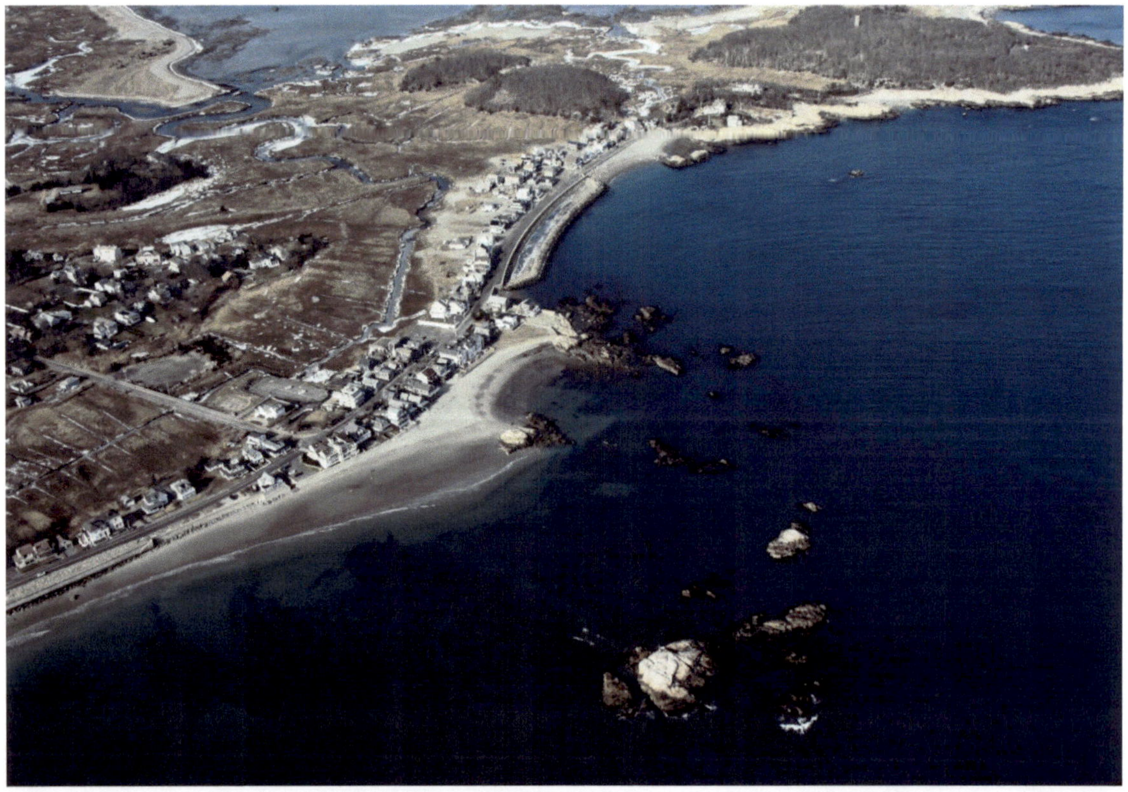

4 Minot Beach, north of center, has resident parking with sticker allowed in town lot left of center. Well Rock in center (below crescent beach). [1/26/18]

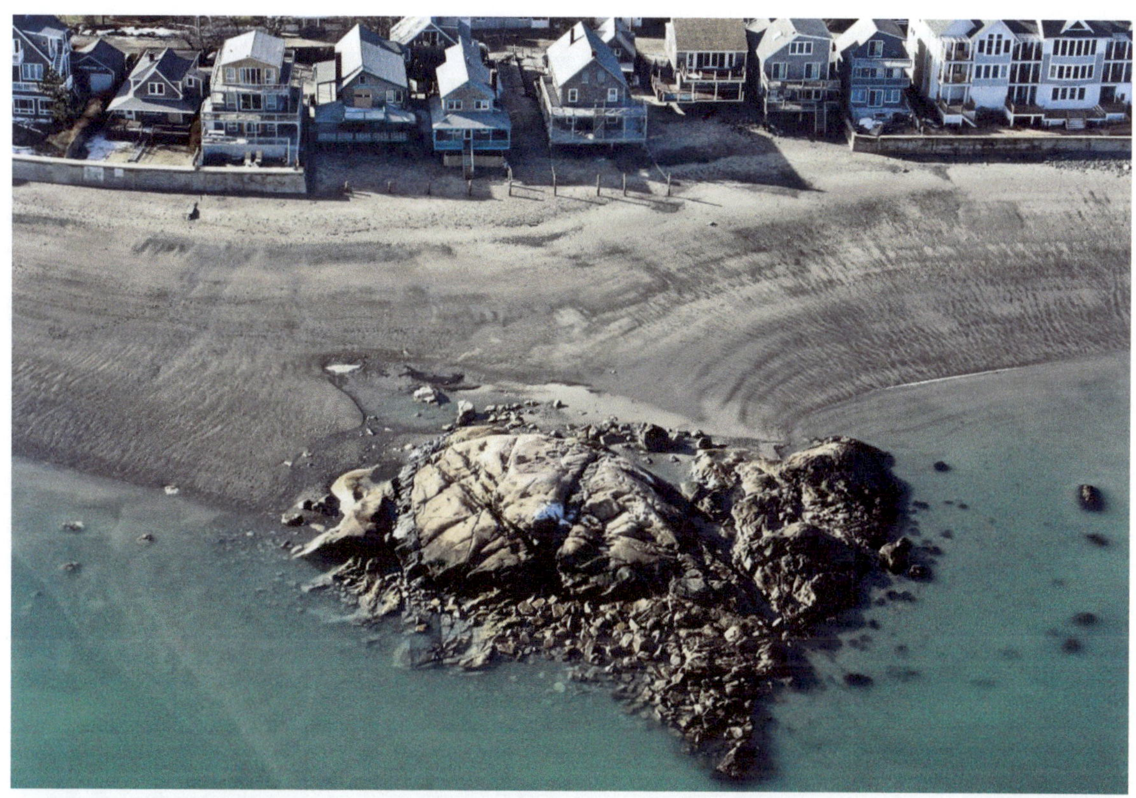

5 Well Rock, Minot Beach, North Scituate. [12/31/10]

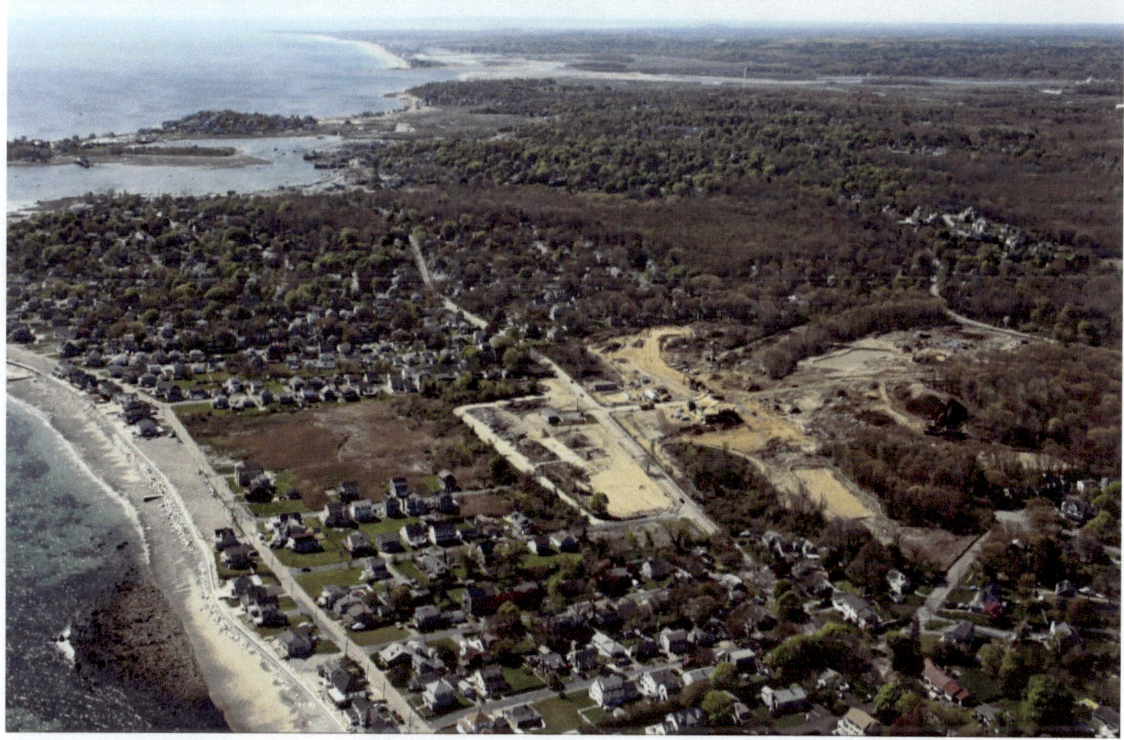

6 Panorama of seacoast with Scituate Harbor, Cliffs, and North River in background. At left, areas known as Oceanside and Sand Hills. At right, early construction of Toll Brothers development, Seaside at Scituate, along Hatherly Road between 6th Ave. and 11th Ave., at former World War I proving ground. [5/10/19]

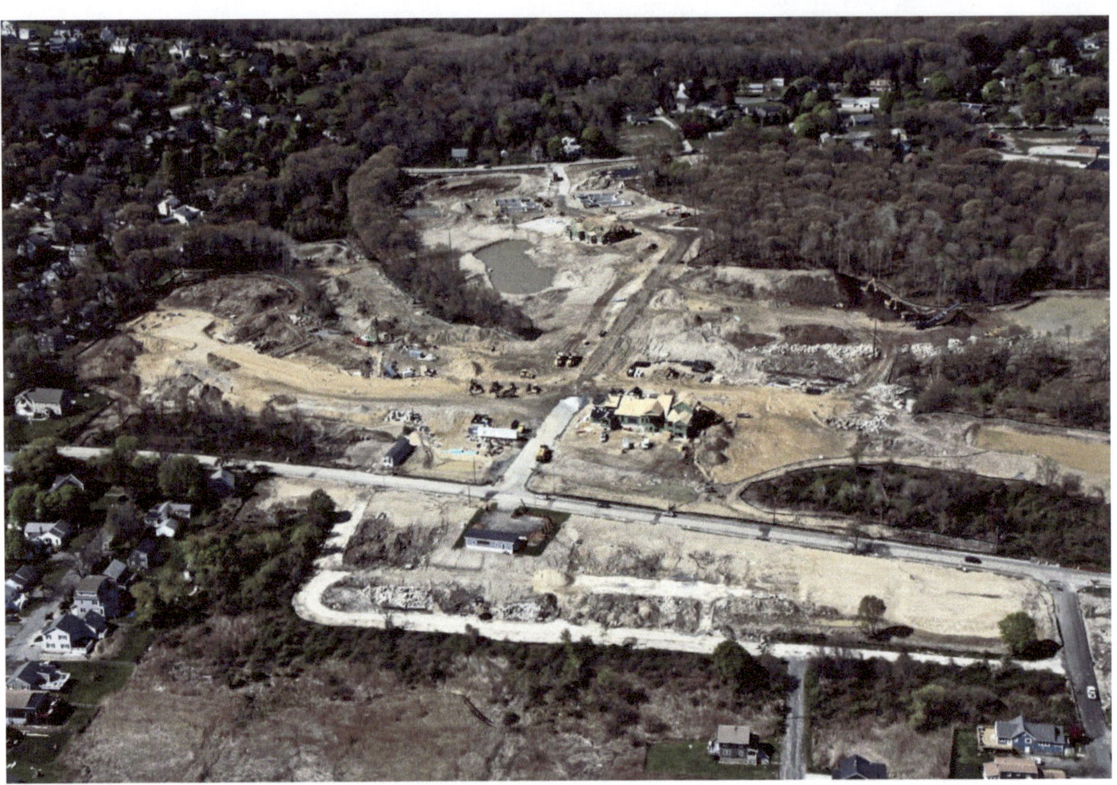

7 Construction underway for Seaside at Scituate. Hatherly Road runs across photo. [5/10/19]

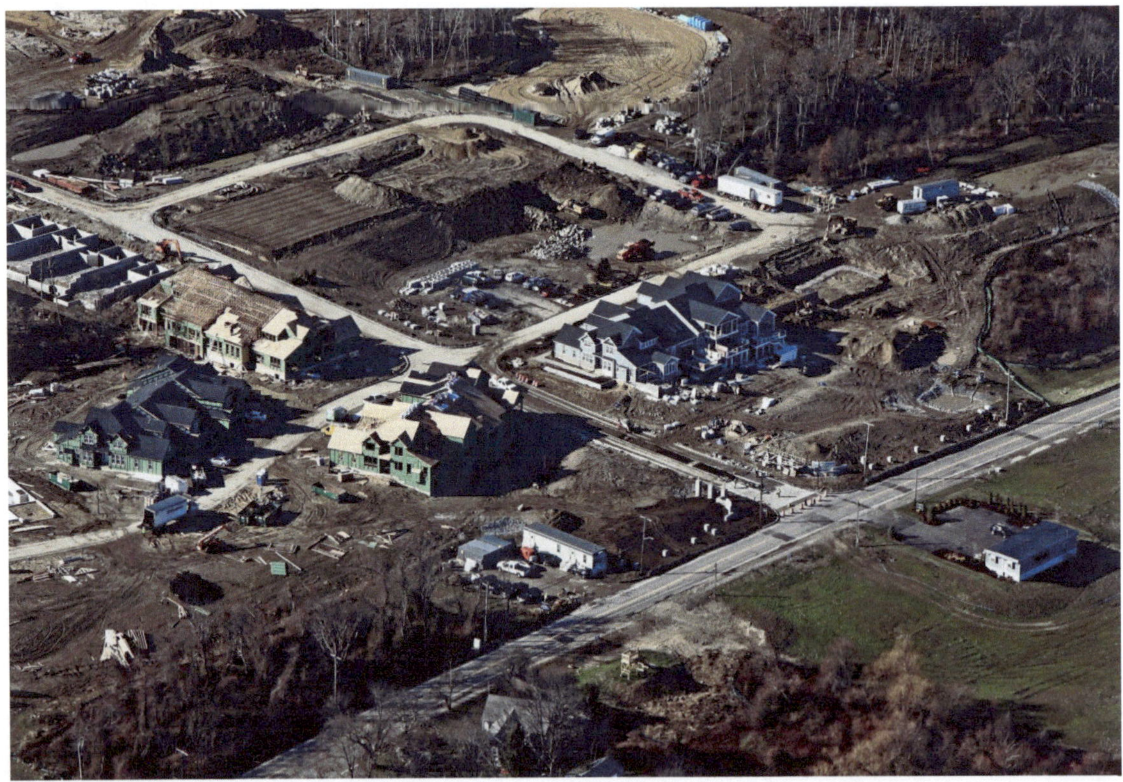

8 Construction underway for Seaside at Scituate. Hatherly Road in foreground. [11/21/19]

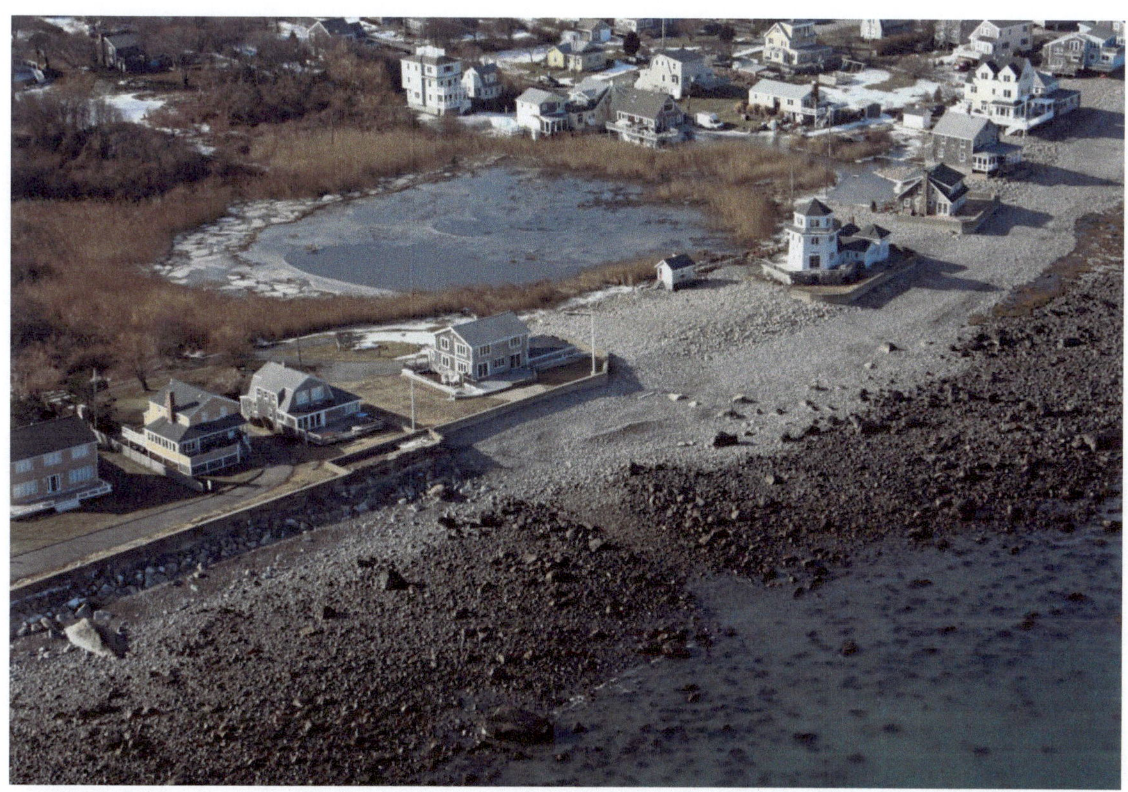

9 Shore Acres. Streets named for Pilgrims (Standish, Carver, Bradford, Alden, and Priscilla Avenues). Hexagonal house on Brewster Ave. at Seaside Road. [12/31/10]

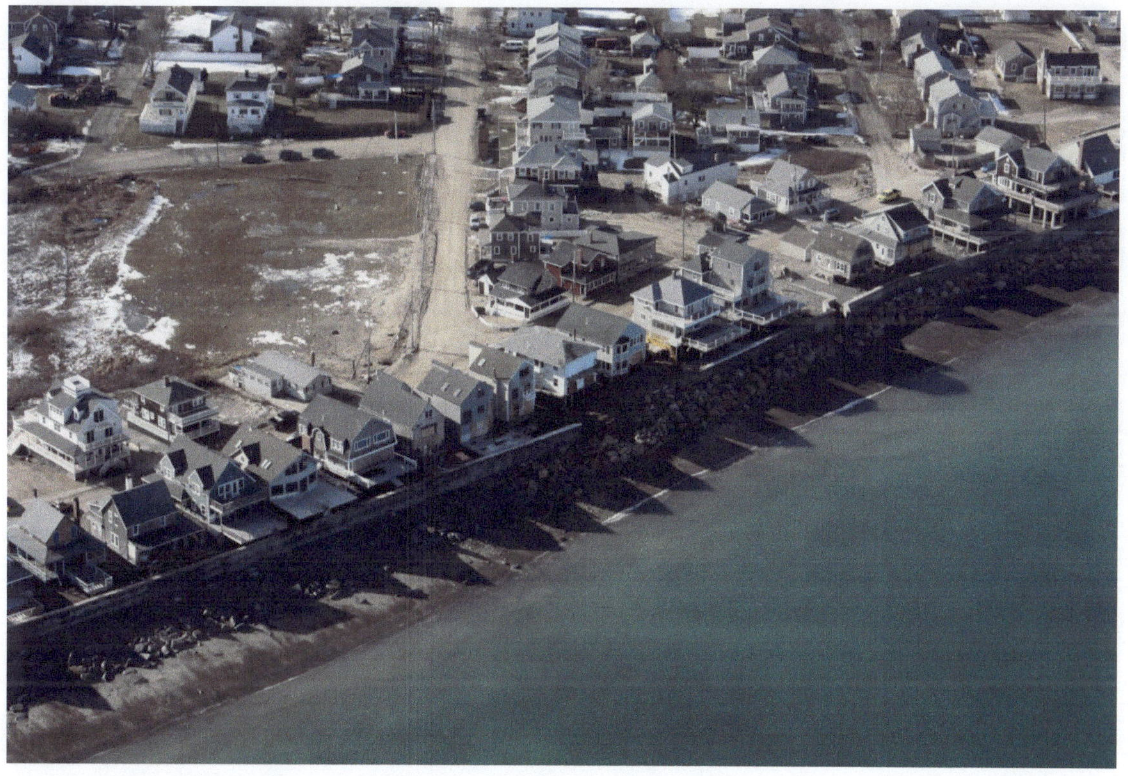

10 Sand Hills. Turner Road at Oceanside Drive. [12/31/10]

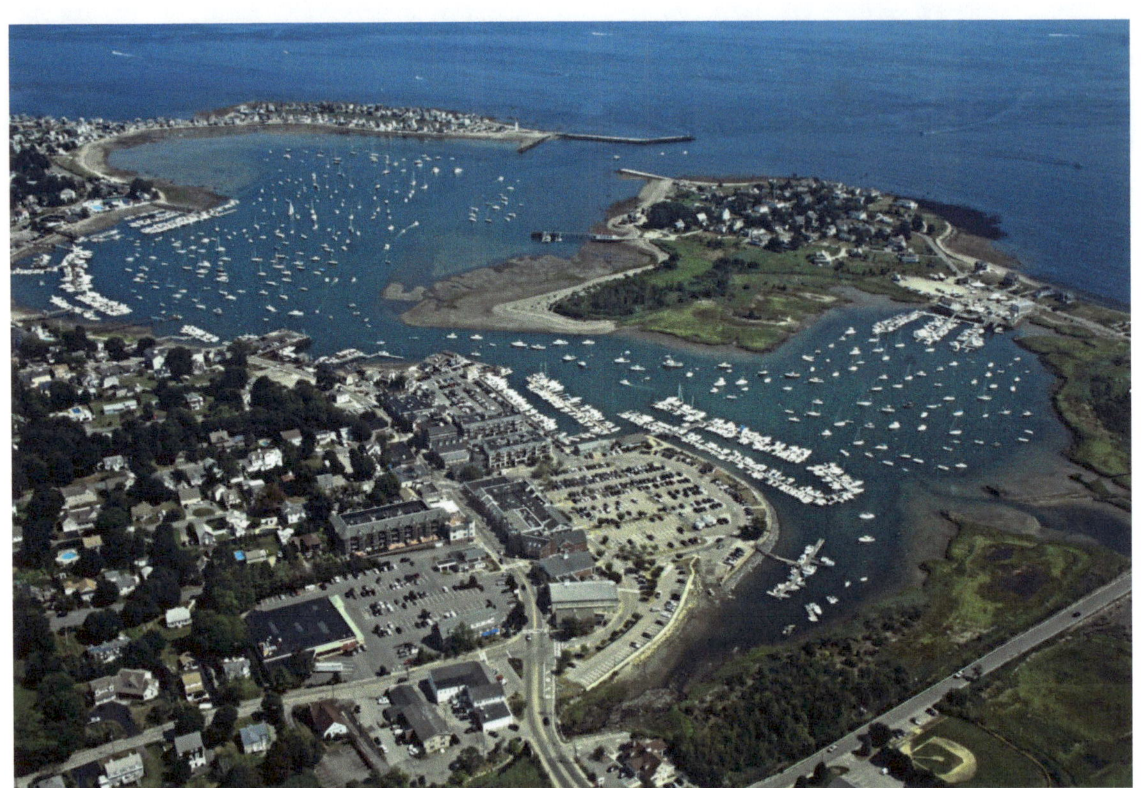

1 Scituate Harbor — the village and the harbor. Entrance (top) between Cedar Point & First Cliff. [8/12/17]

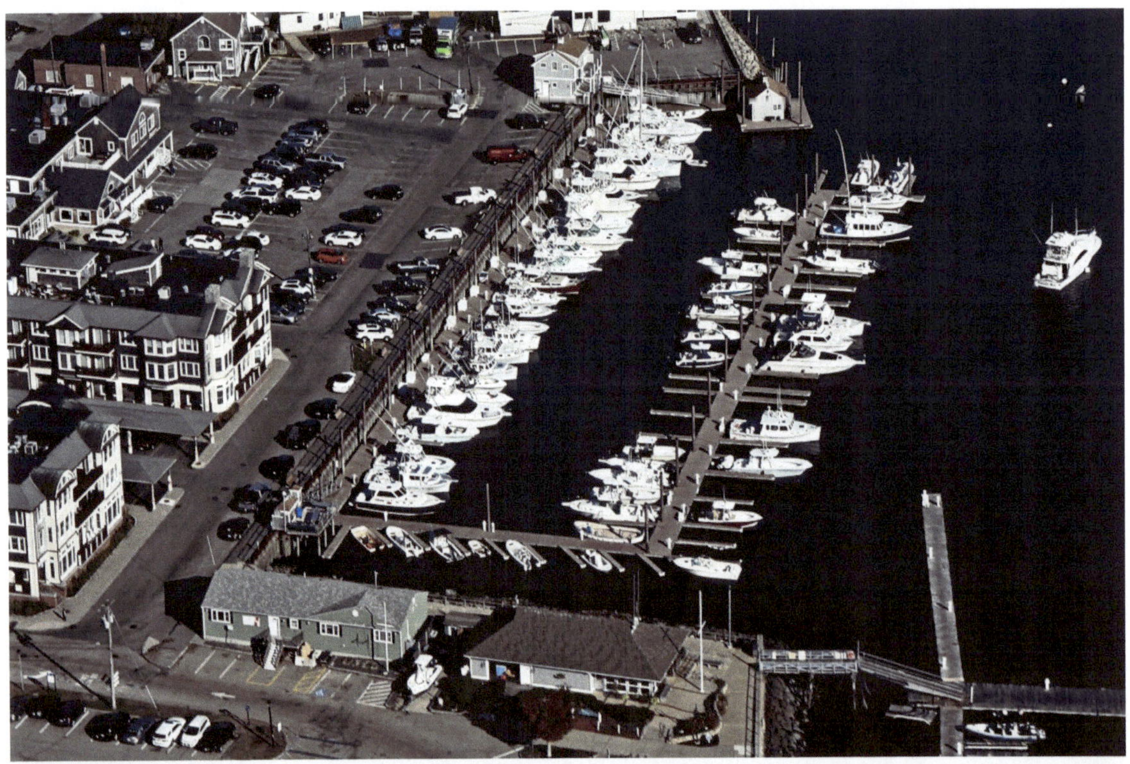

2 Marina in Scituate Harbor near Mill Wharf. In foreground, offices of US Coast Guard (left) and Scituate Harbormaster. [10/18/19]

3

SCITUATE HARBOR, CEDAR POINT, FIRST CLIFF

Scituate Harbor, Cedar Point (Lighthouse Point), and First Cliff are shown on the cover of this book. Previous history books have documented these places well, including Barbara Murphy's book, *Irish Mossers and Scituate Harbour Village*.[11]

Scituate has abundant marine resources, including NOAA, US Coast Guard, Town Pier and other commercial fishing piers, Scituate Marine Park and Maritime Center, Scituate Harbormaster's office, and multiple marinas. The Lucien Rousseau Memorial Landing at the southern end of Cole Parkway — named for the buyer of Irish moss — is a private dock for fishing vessels and skiffs.[12]

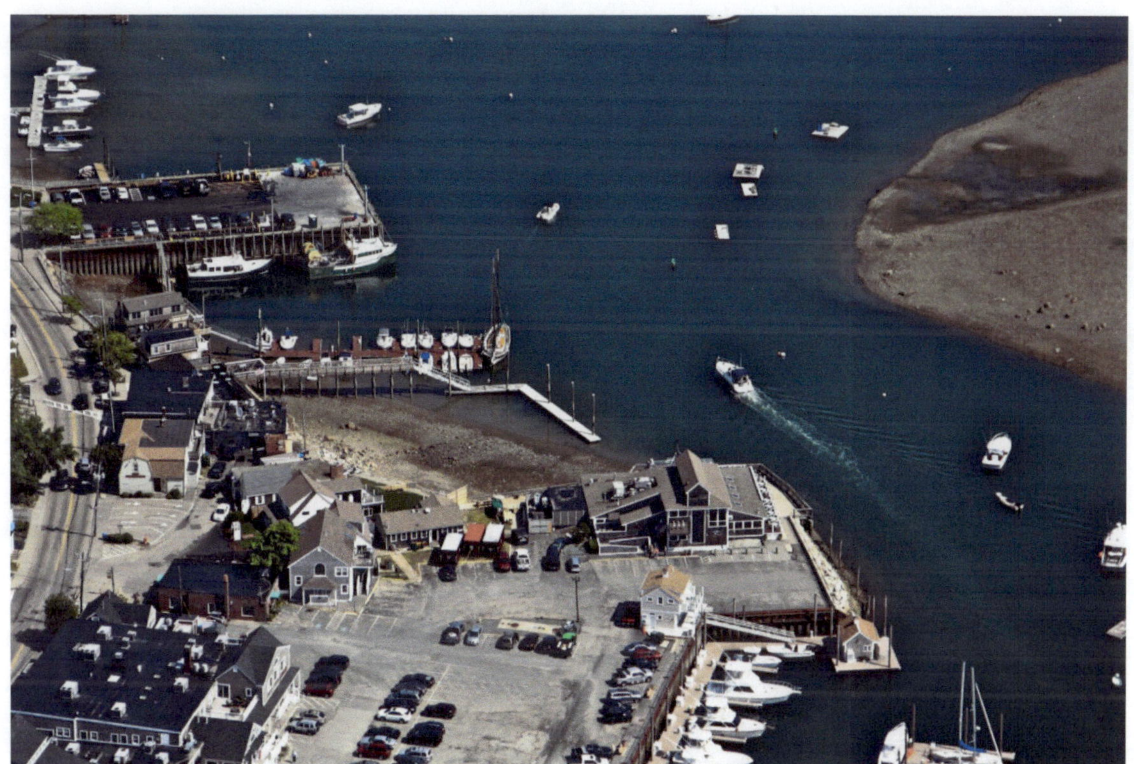

3 Town Pier (top left) and Mill Wharf restaurant (foreground, right) at Scituate harbor. [6/6/15]

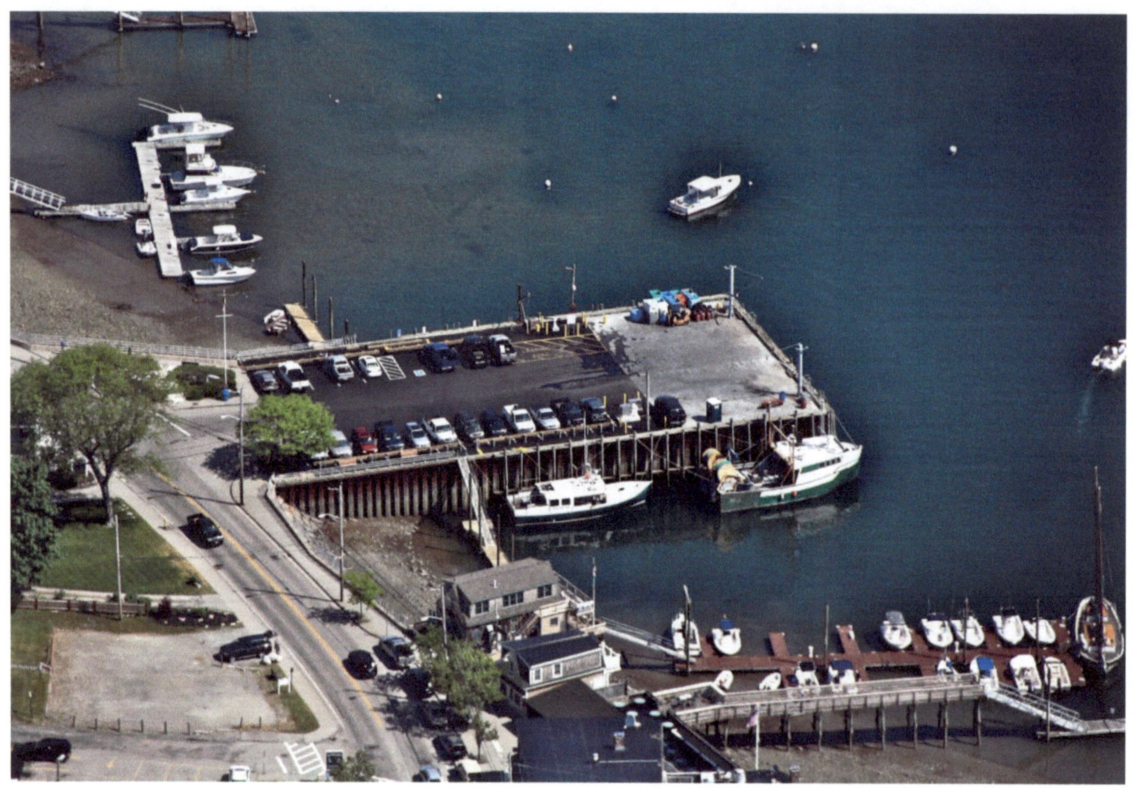

4 Town Pier, used for commercial fishing. [6/6/15]

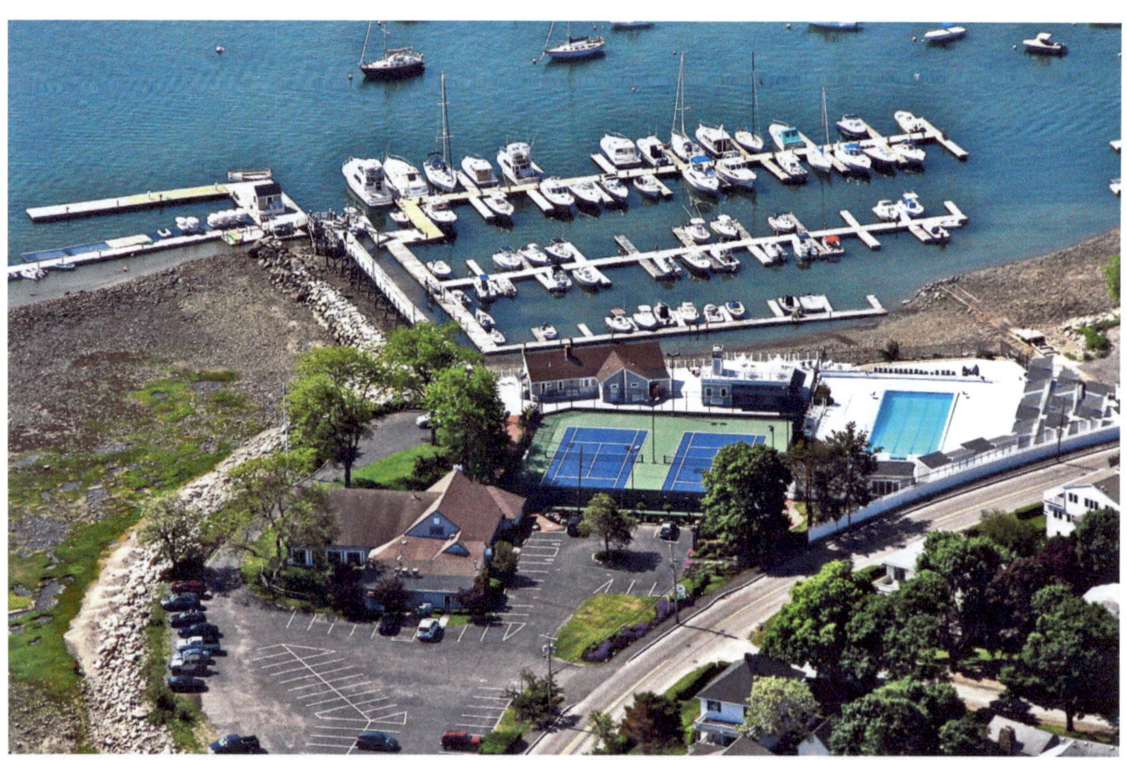

5 Scituate Harbor Yacht Club. [6/6/15]

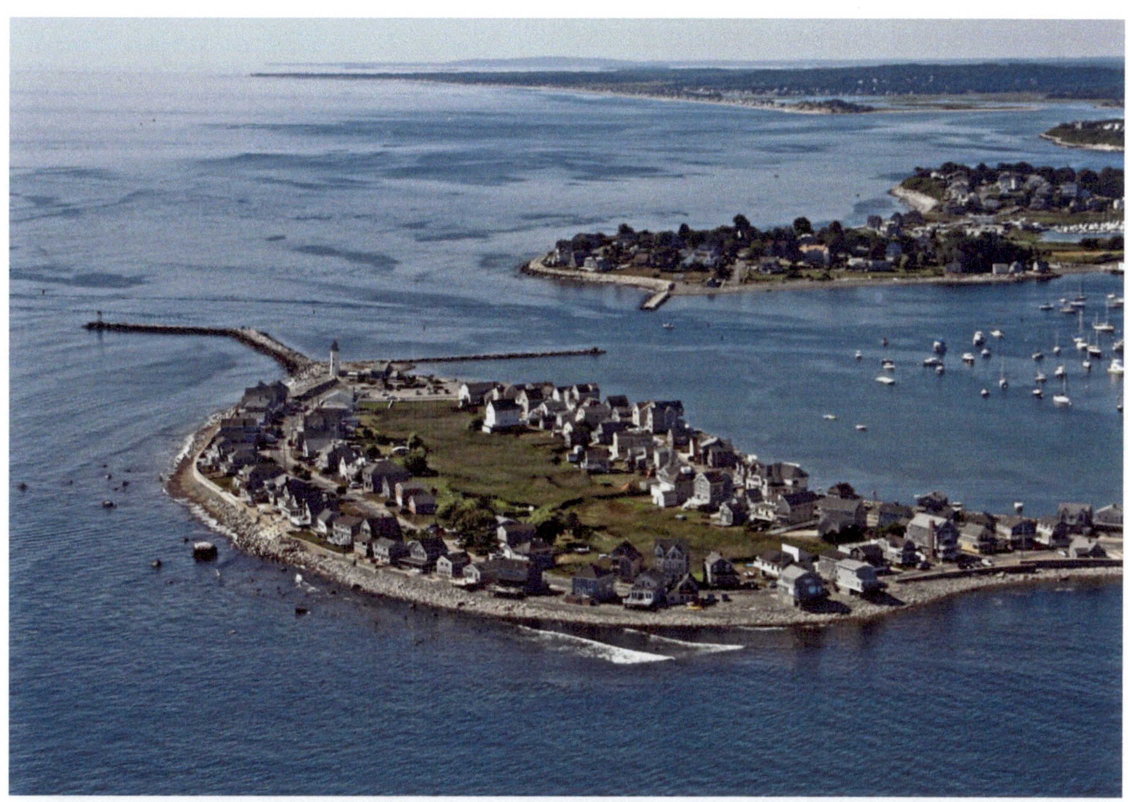

6 Panorama of coast, looking south, with Cedar Point (Lighthouse Point) and Scituate Harbor in foreground, then First, Second, and Third Cliffs, North River, Fourth Cliff, and Marshfield. [7/15/16]

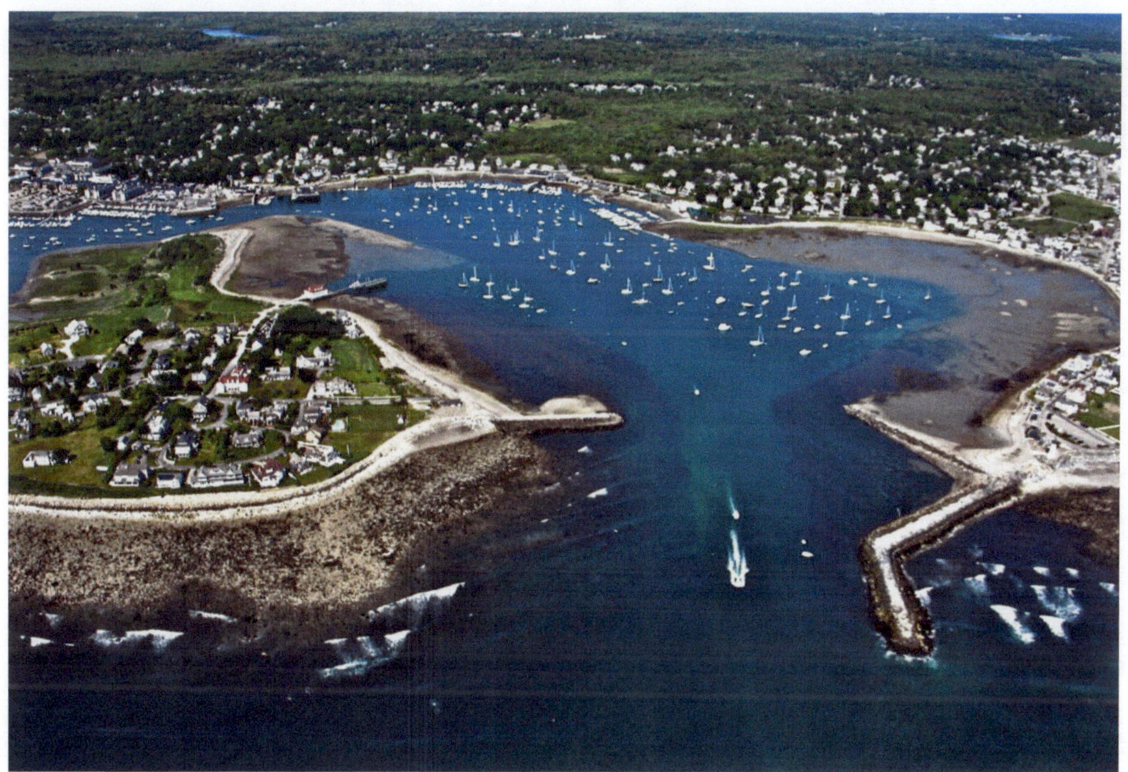

7 Another view of Scituate harbor, looking west, with First Cliff on left and Cedar Point on right. [6/6/15]

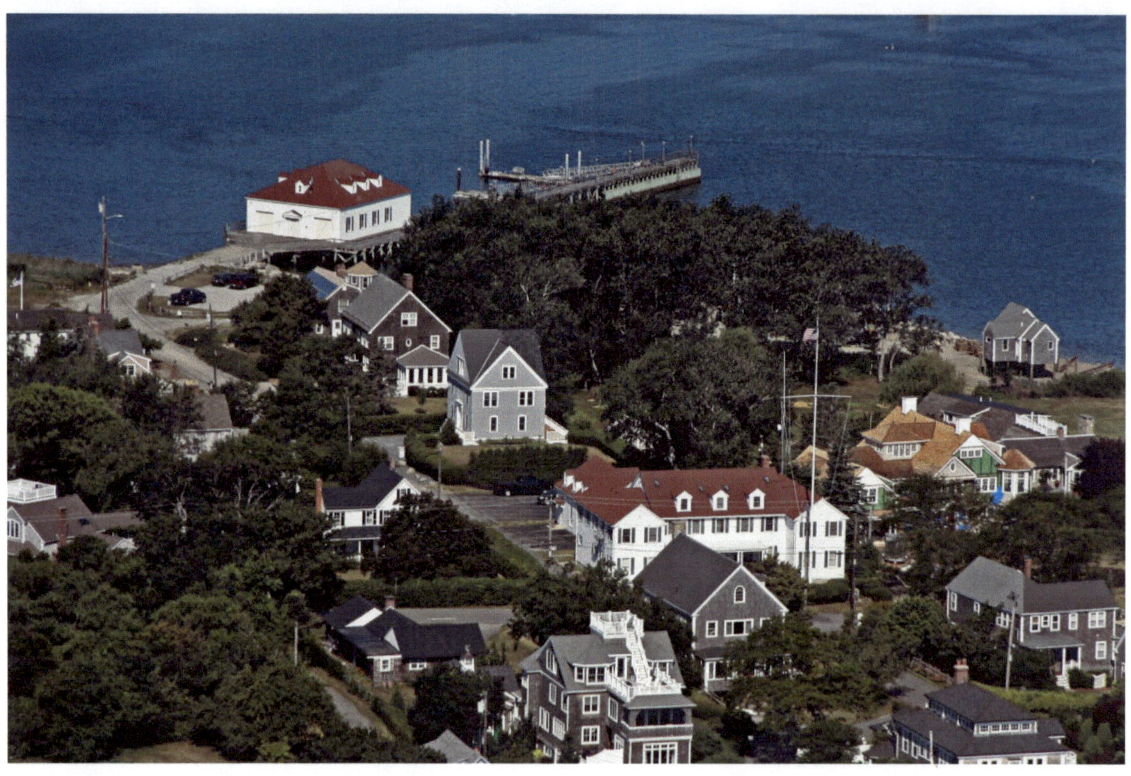

8 At First Cliff, two red-roofed buildings and wharf are those of NOAA (National Oceanic and Atmospheric Administration); both were the original US Coast Guard Station Scituate. [7/15/16]

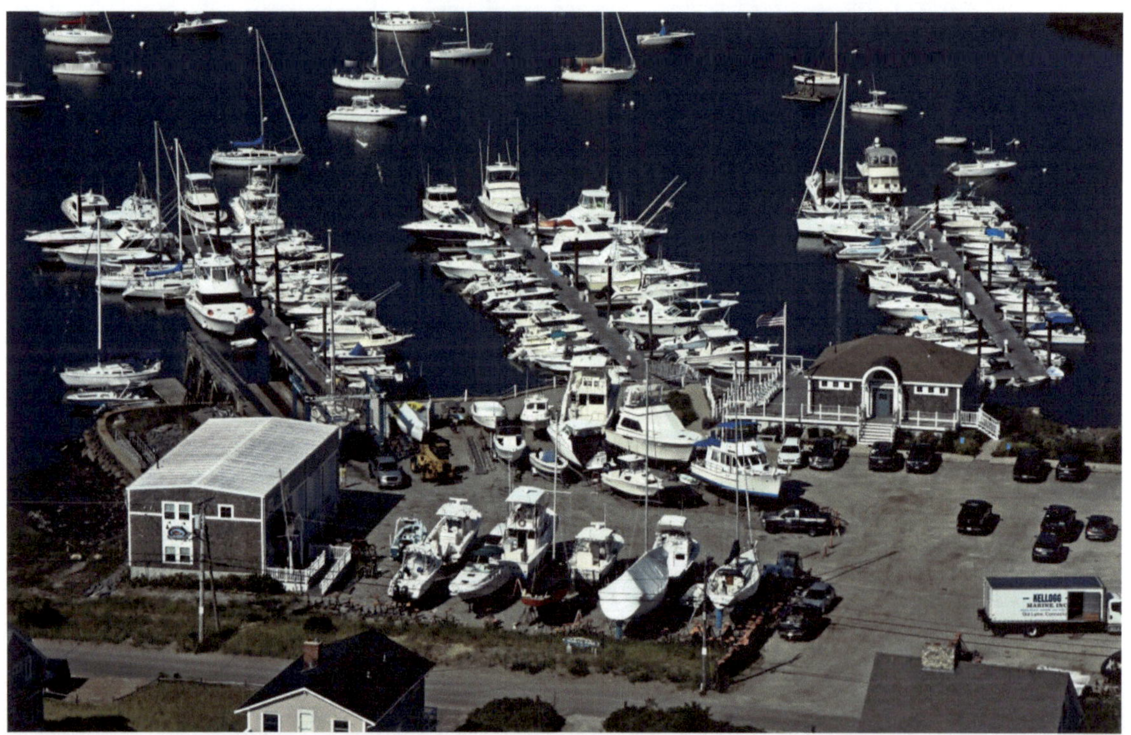

9 At First Cliff, Scituate Marine Park and Maritime Center includes boatyard, municipal marina, and Maritime Center meeting place (building, center right). [8/29/18]

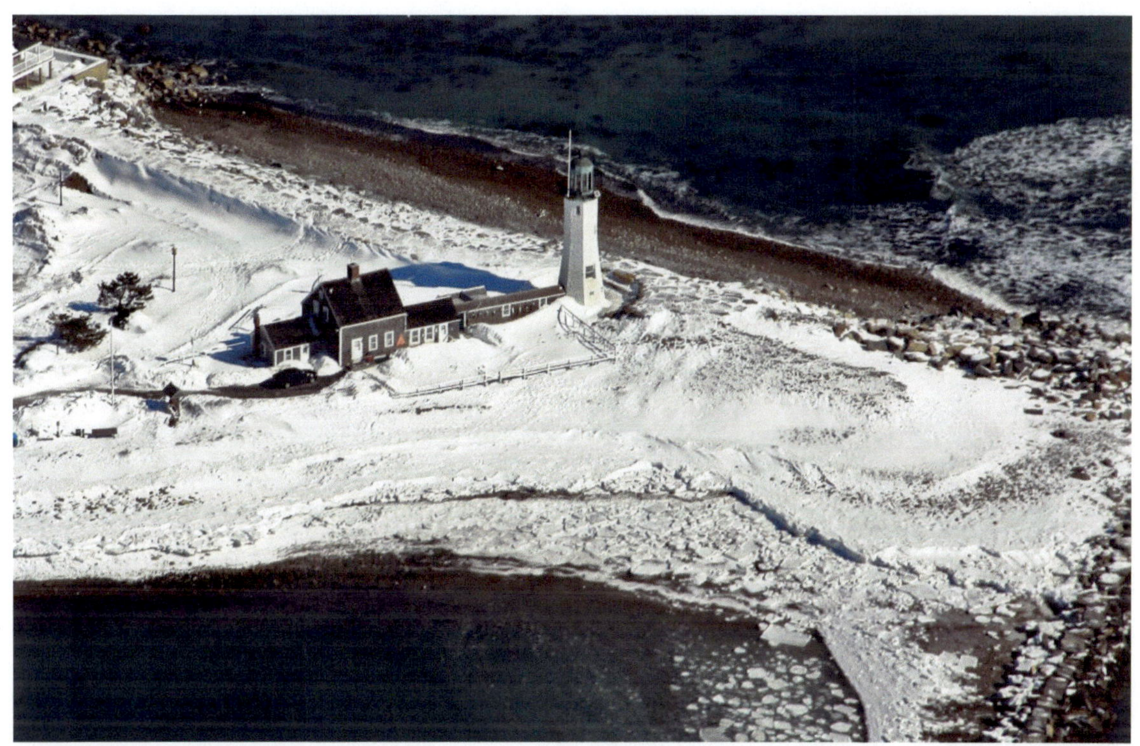

10 Old Scituate Light (1811) in winter. [2/27/15]

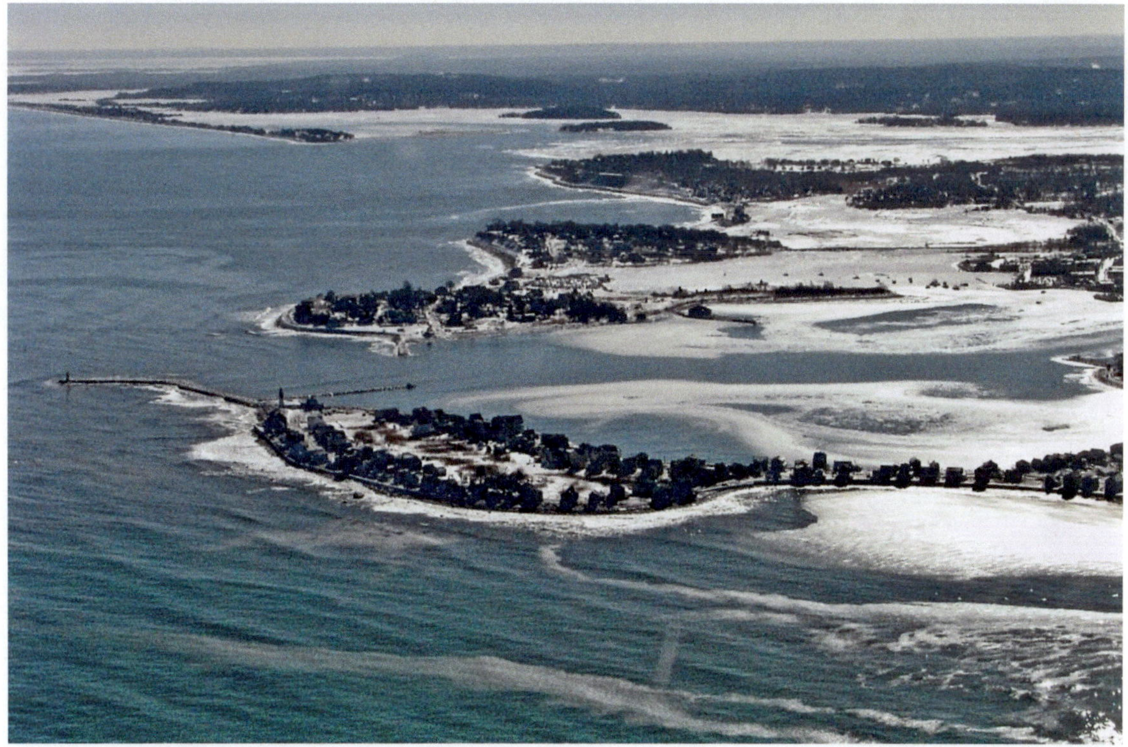

11 Cedar Point and the Cliffs in winter, ice in the harbor. [1/29/05]

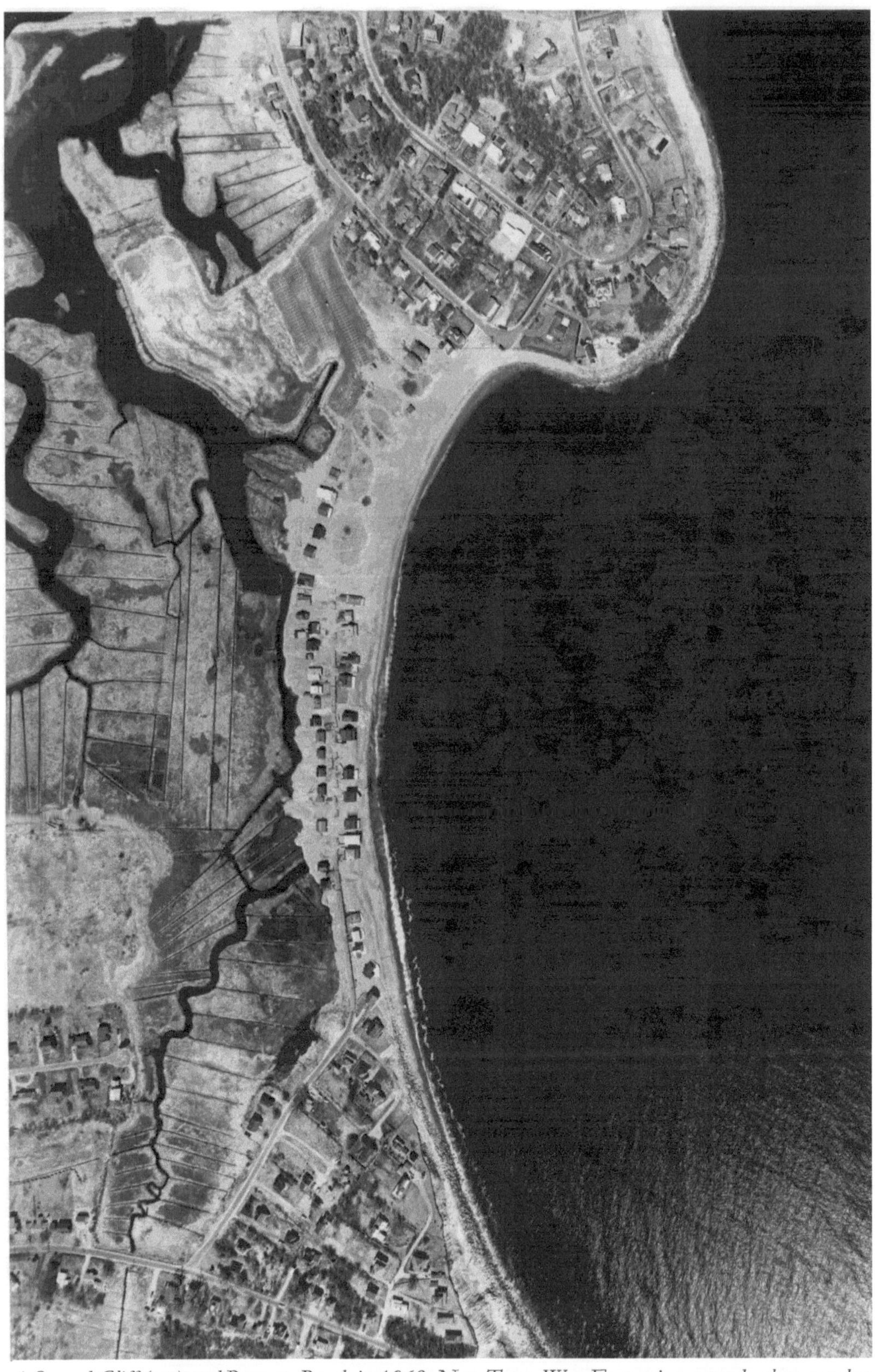

1 Second Cliff (top) and Peggotty Beach in 1968. Note Town Way Extension extends along southern half of the beach, with cottages on both sides. Source: Town of Scituate, Town Archives, CGL-134.

4

SECOND CLIFF, PEGGOTTY BEACH

Second Cliff became a popular destination for summer visitors in the early 1900s. Peggotty Beach, named for a character in a Charles Dickens novel, connects Second Cliff with Third Cliff. Both cliffs are reached by the Edward Foster Memorial Bridge.[13]

Second Cliff was a particular summer home for early 1900s activists for women's right to vote. The most notable suffragist was Inez Haynes Irwin, who helped start college equal suffrage leagues and who wrote the history of the National Women's Party. But a surprising number of other nationally known suffragists spent summers at Lighthouse Point, Second Cliff, and Third Cliff. For more on the suffragists, see Lyle Nyberg's book, *Summer Suffragists*.[14]

Peggotty Beach was a popular place for the industry of gathering Irish moss, a seaweed used as a thickening agent in foods, ice cream, and beer. Irish mossers would row out in dories (boats) and use long-handled rakes to gather the moss from rocks under the sea at low tide. The moss was spread out on beaches to dry. Scituate was a national capital for the industry, which lasted from the mid-1800s to the late 1900s.[15]

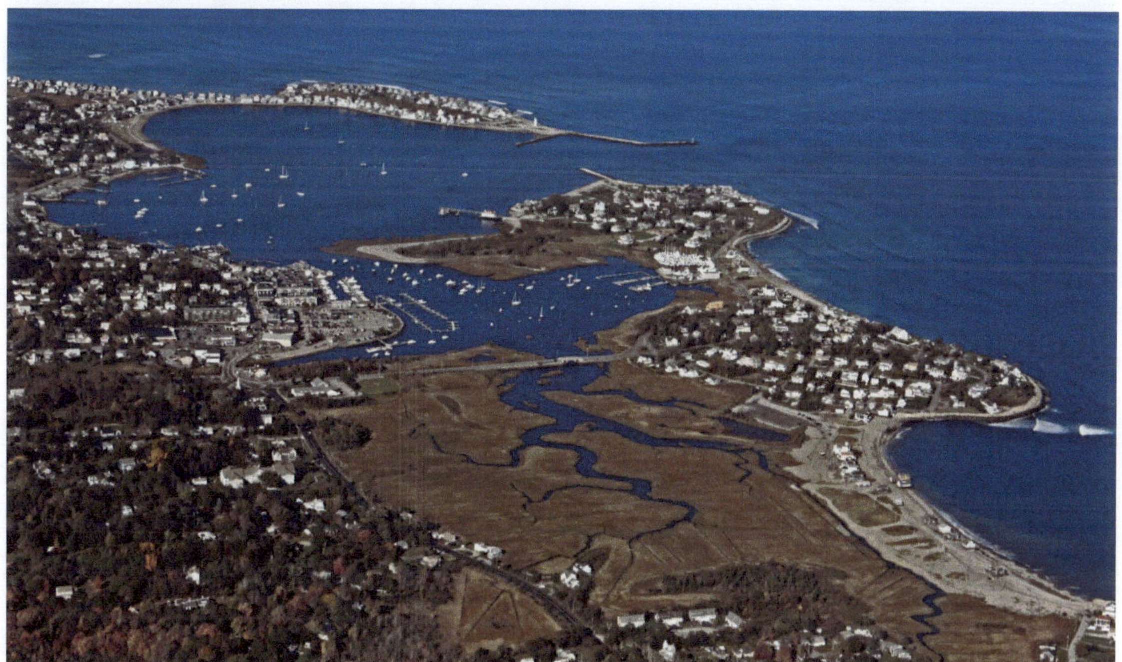

2 Panorama of Scituate harbor, with Scituate Harbor village at left, Cedar Point at top, then First Cliff, Second Cliff, and Peggotty Beach (right). [10/27/17]

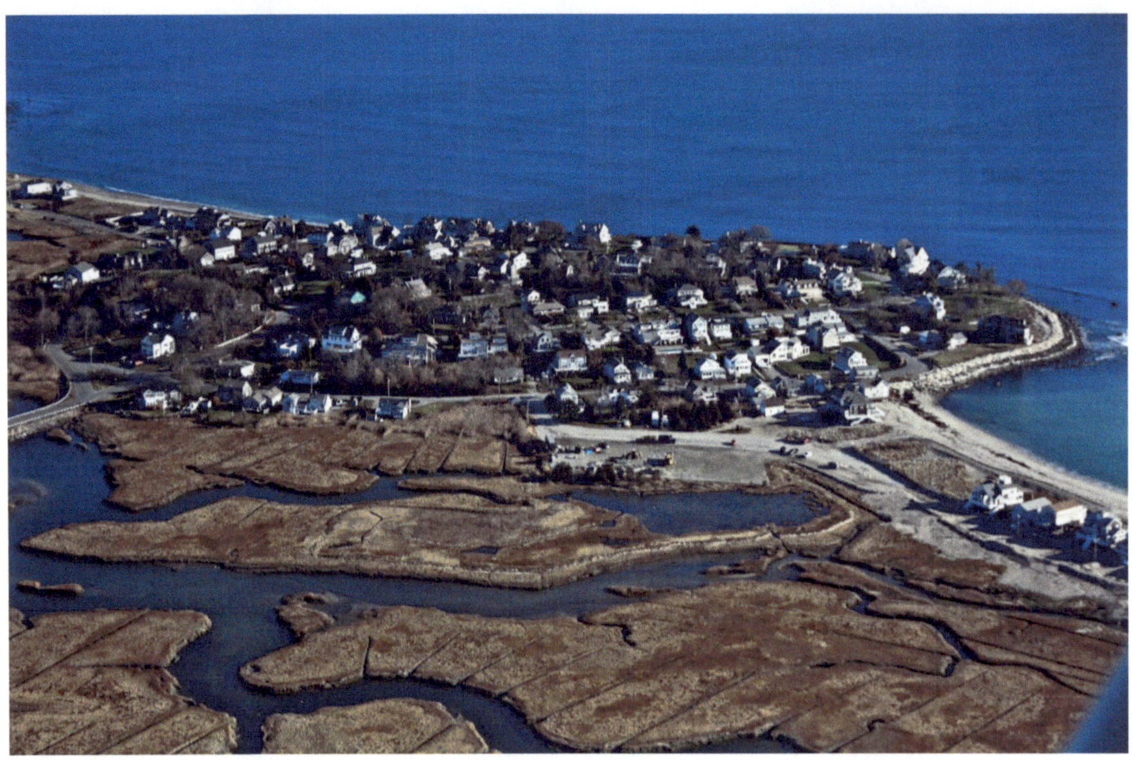

3 Second Cliff, with (from left, in center) Edward Foster Memorial Bridge, Peggotty Beach Road, Peggotty Beach. [12/4/15]

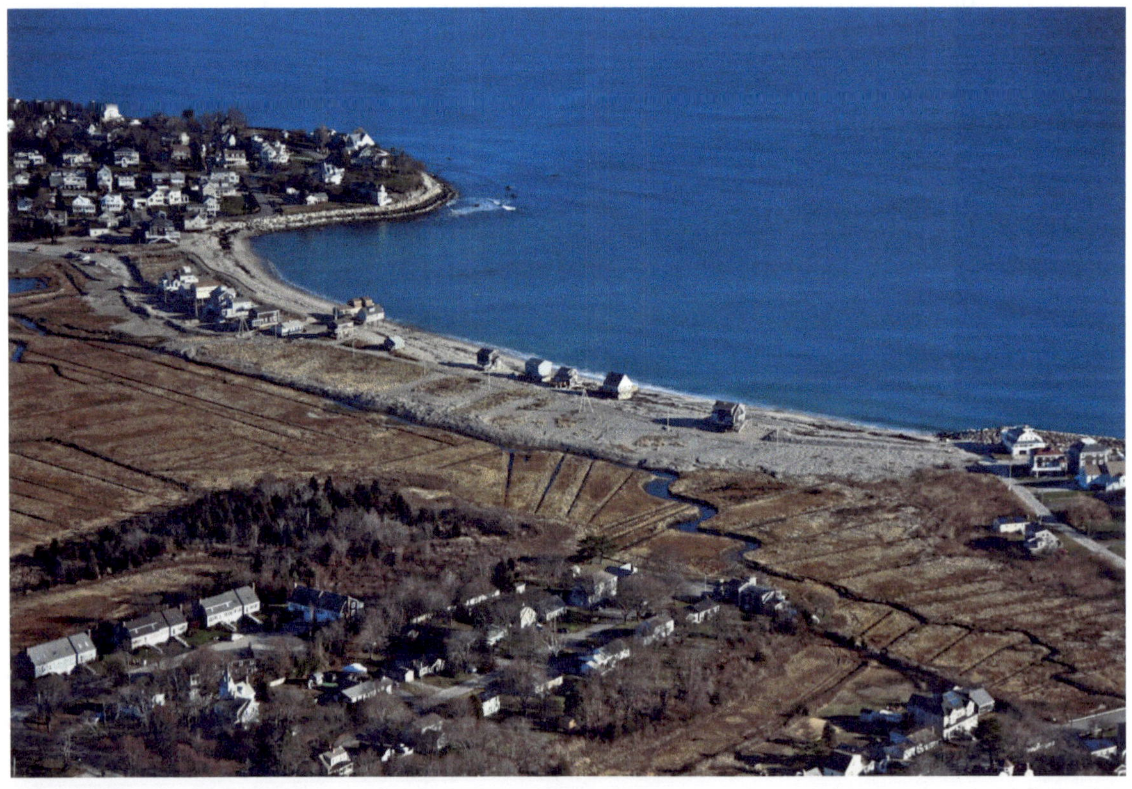

4 Peggotty Beach, looking east, with Second Cliff (top left). [12/4/15]

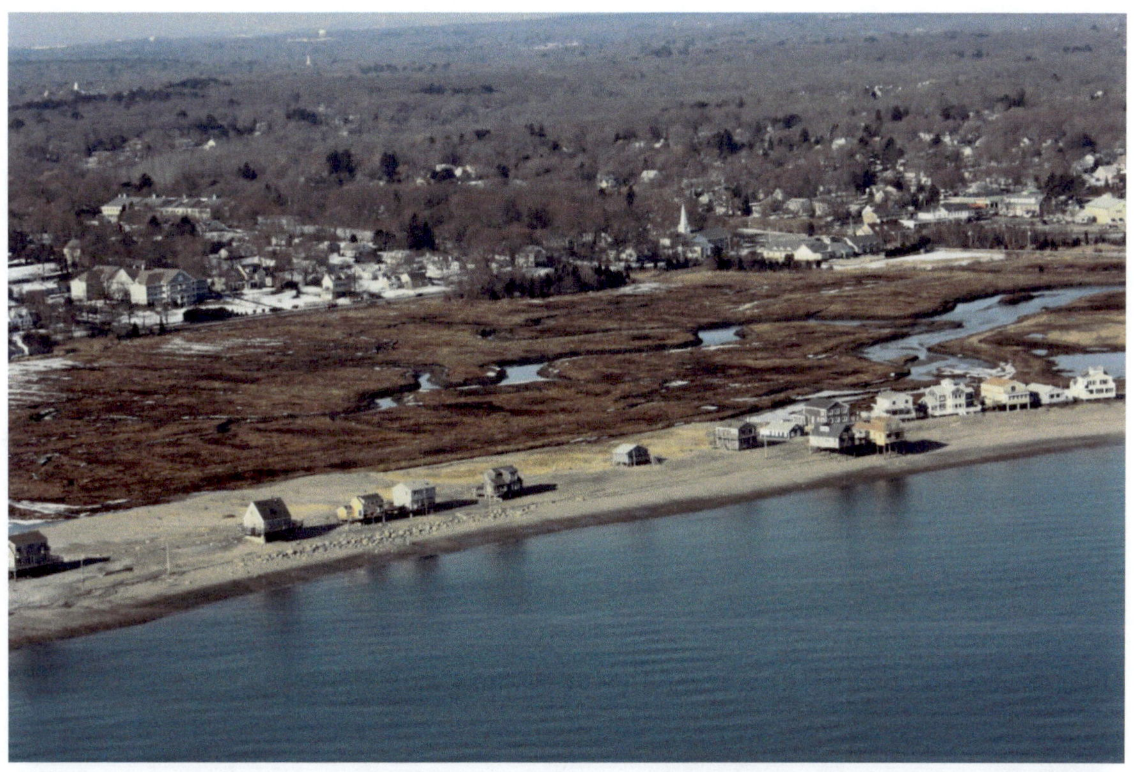

5 Peggotty Beach, looking west, with Kent Street running across center of photo. Meeting House Estate condos (far left), St. Mary of the Nativity church (spire, right of center), Scituate Harbor (right). [12/31/10]

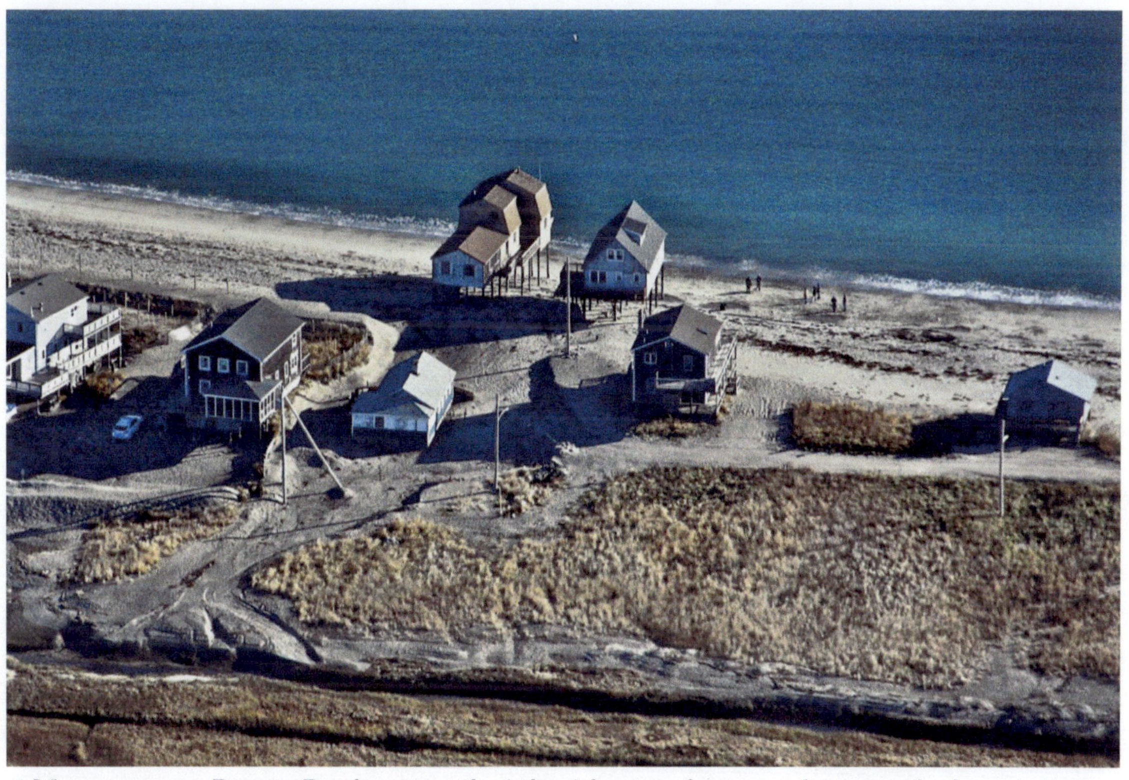

6 Many cottages at Peggotty Beach are on stilts (pilings) because of storms and rising sea levels. [12/4/15]

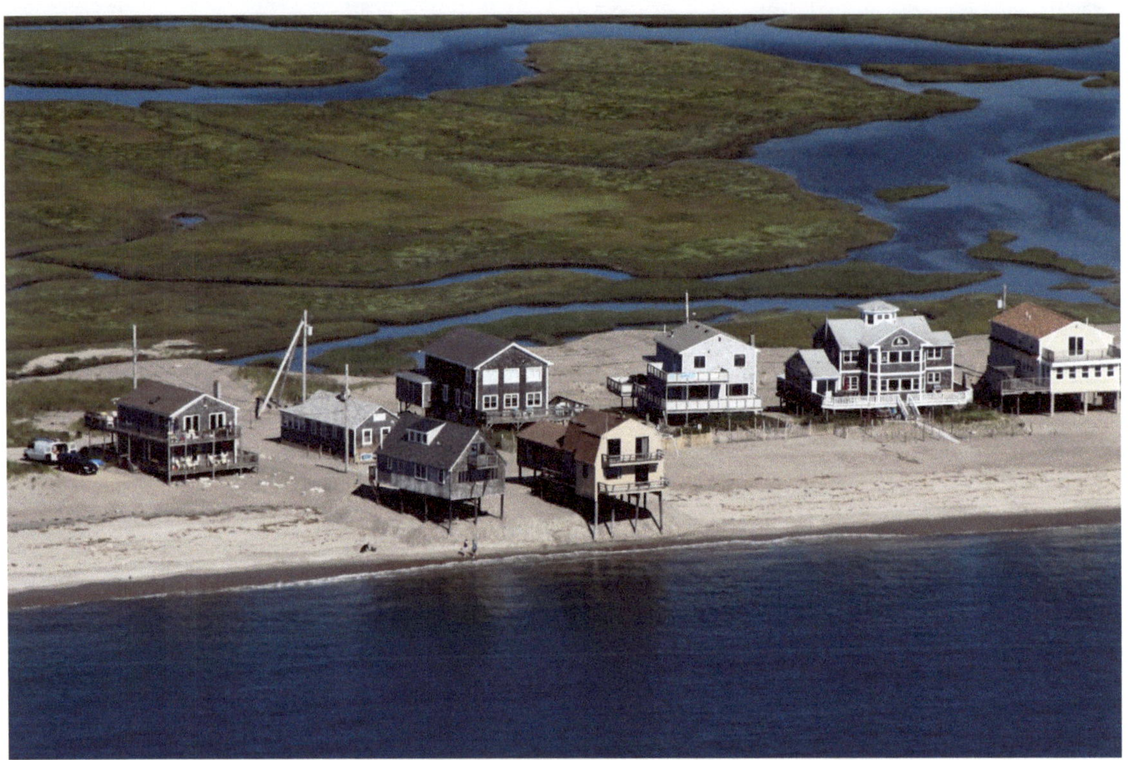

7 Cottages between ocean and marsh on Peggotty Beach, a barrier beach. [7/15/16]

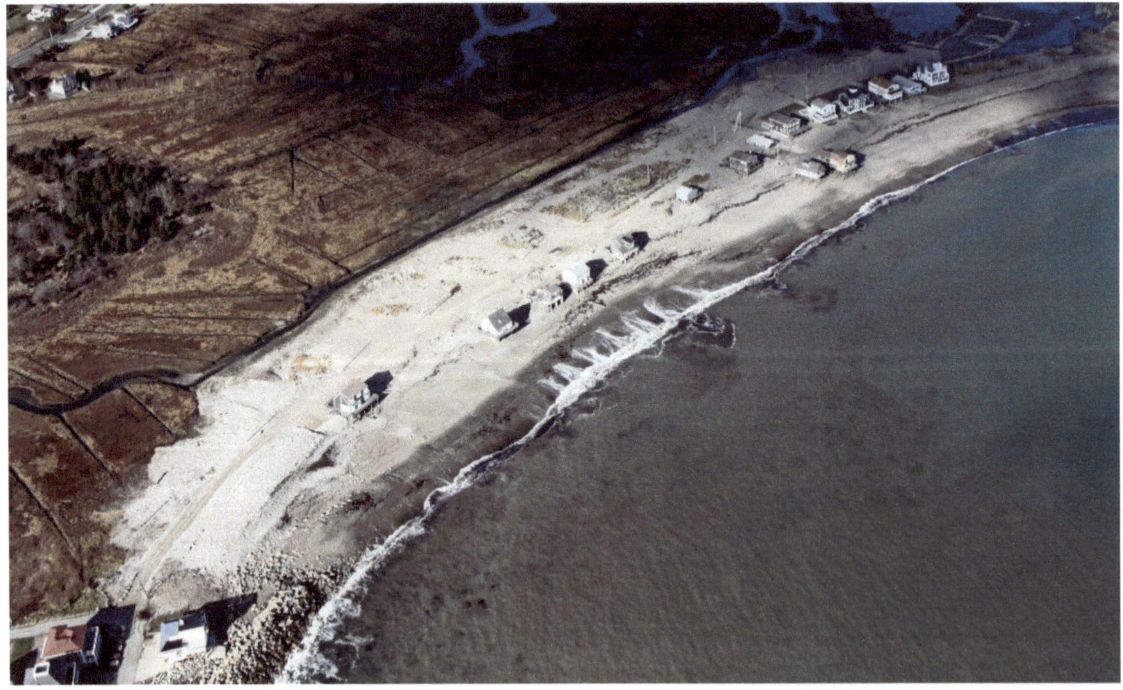

8 Peggotty Beach, southern end. [11/29/18]

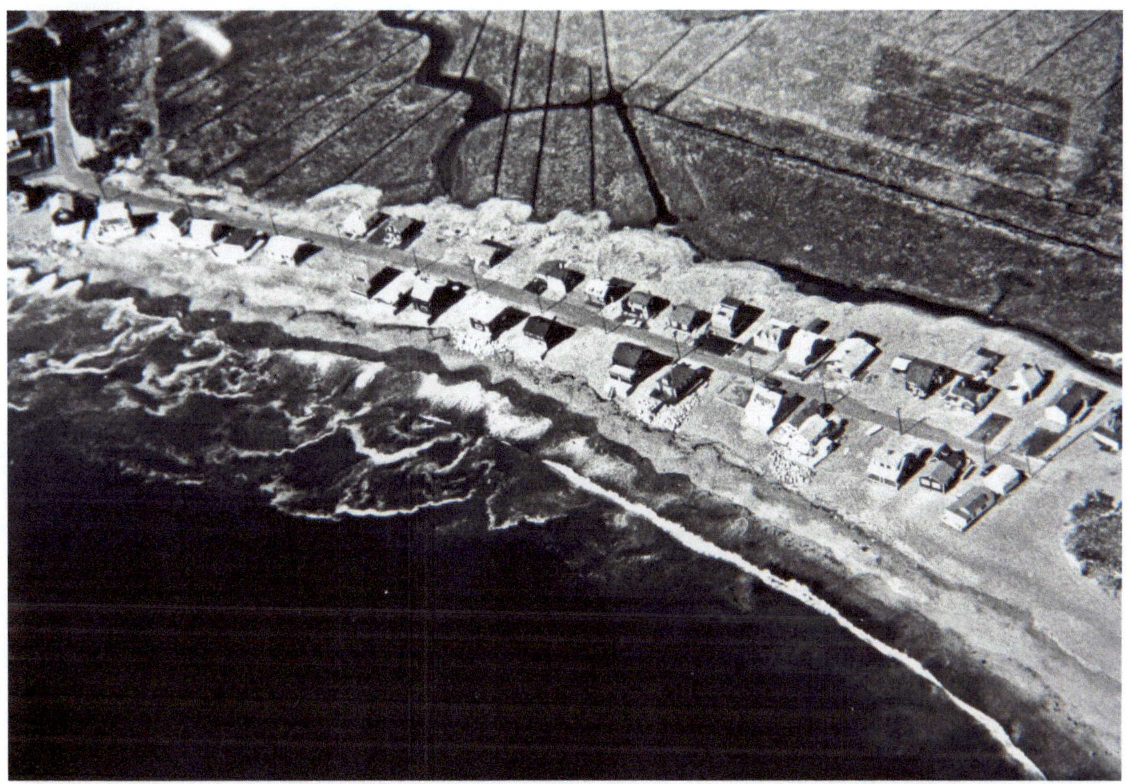

9 Peggotty Beach, southern end, 1976. Town Way Extension with cottages on both sides. [July 1976]

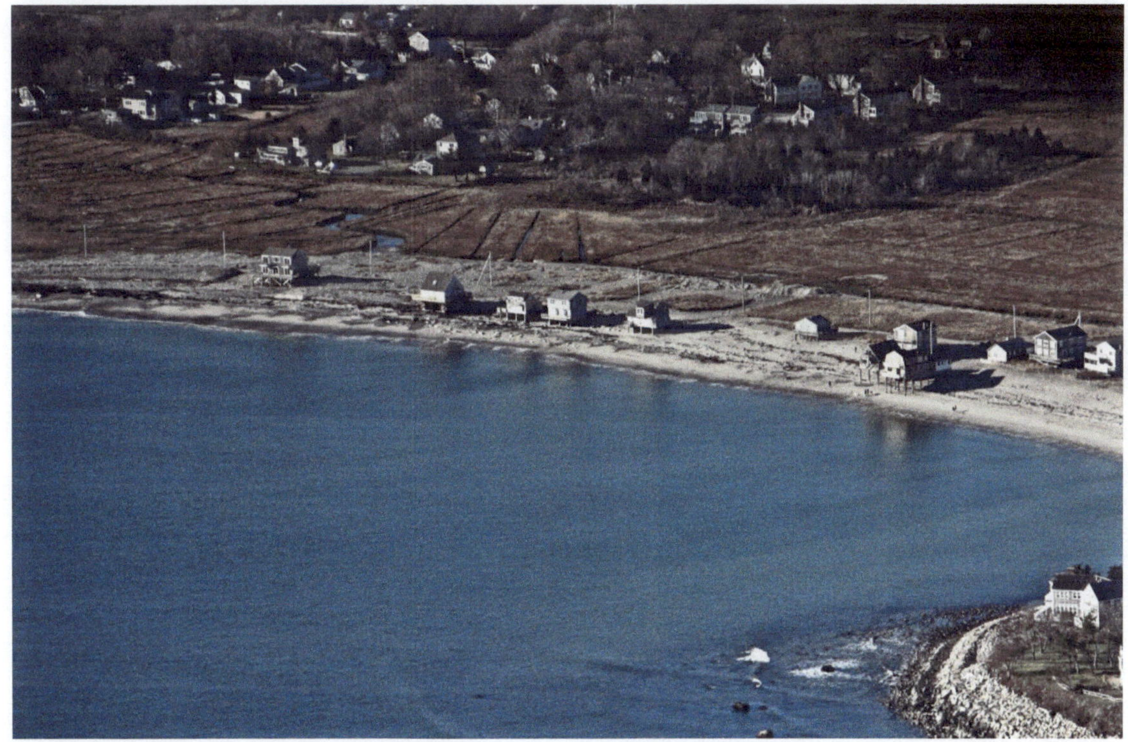

10 Peggotty Beach, part of Second Cliff on the right. Few cottages remain after Blizzard of 1978. [12/4/15]

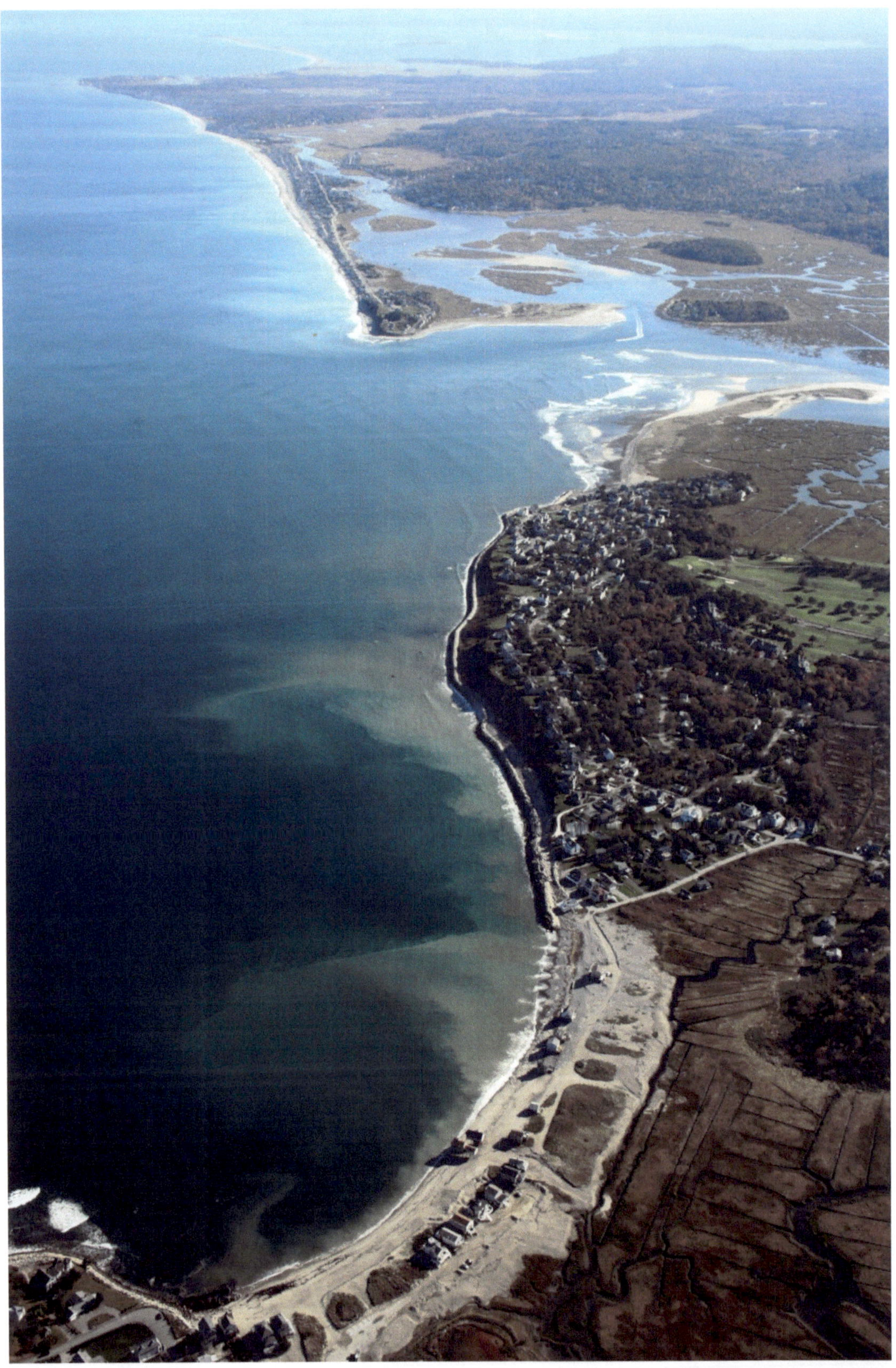

1 Looking south. From bottom, Peggotty Beach, Third Cliff, North River, Fourth Cliff/Humarock.
[10/27/17]

5

THIRD CLIFF, THE DRIFTWAY

Third Cliff has a deep and wide place in Scituate's history. Here were colonial-era farms that were transformed in the early 1900s into summer colonies and the Scituate Country Club, as explored in more detail in Lyle Nyberg's book *On a Cliff*. From this shore, Irish immigrants and their descendants made Scituate the American capital of Irish moss, gathered from the sea and used in many foods and beverages. In addition, Third Cliff is a place of scenic beauty.[16]

Third Cliff is bounded by the ocean, marshes, and rivers including the North River. At the southern end of Third Cliff is the Spit.

The Driftway is a road named in colonial times. It goes from Greenbush to Third Cliff and provides access to Scituate Harbor. It runs near the Herring River, a tributary of the North River. At the Greenbush rotary, it connects with Chief Justice Cushing Highway (Route 3A). That highway travels south, past the new housing at Sanctuary at Herring Brook, and then crosses the North River into Marshfield.[17]

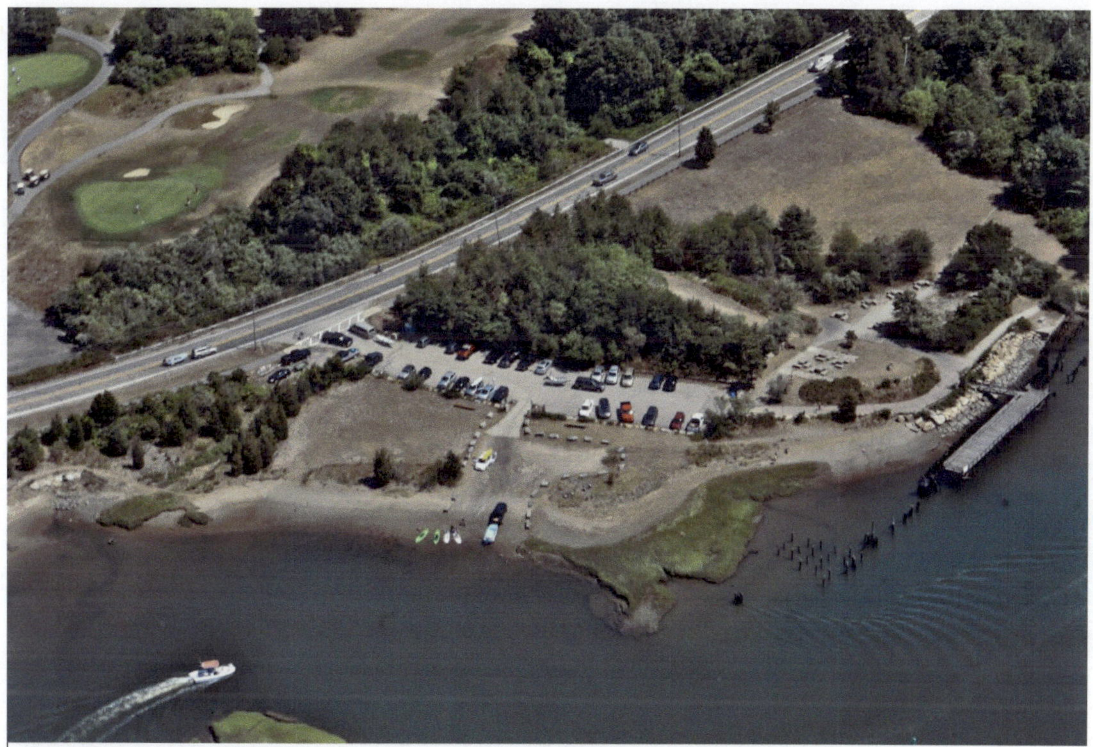

2 Herring River boat launch, the Driftway Conservation Park, part of Widow's Walk golf course (upper left). At lower right are old piers used to load sand from Coleman Hills. [8/13/16]

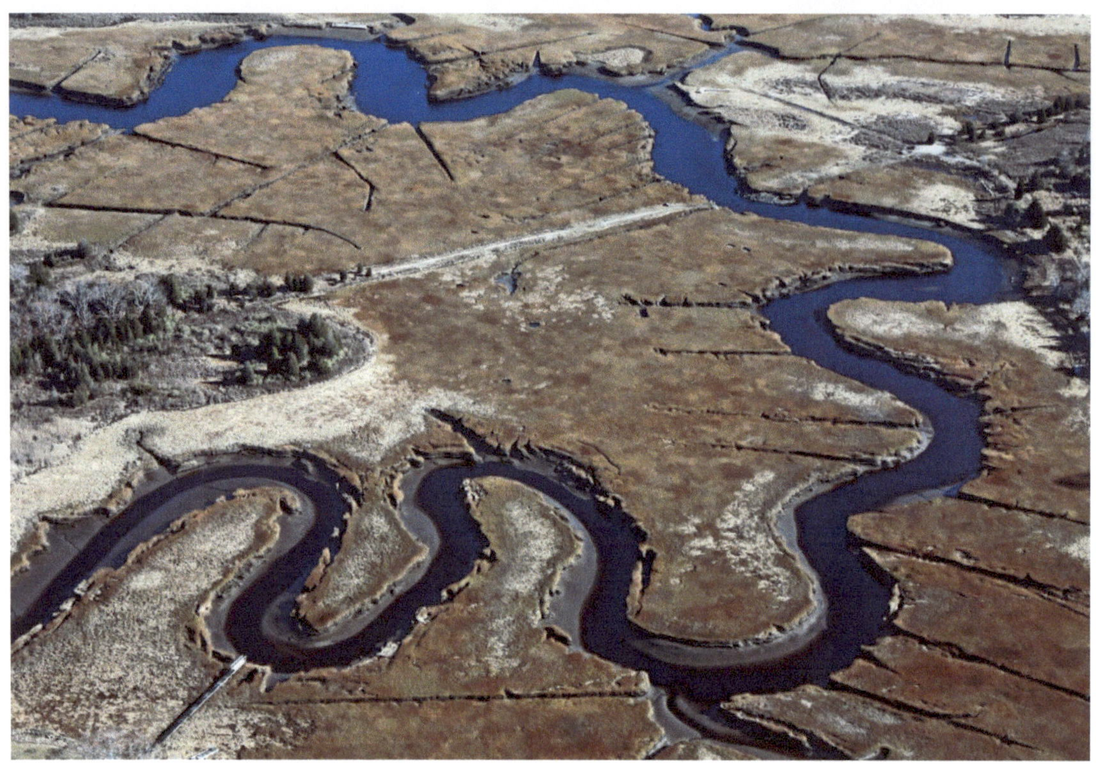

3 Herring River, with trail of Old Colony rail line (light colored line). [11/21/19]

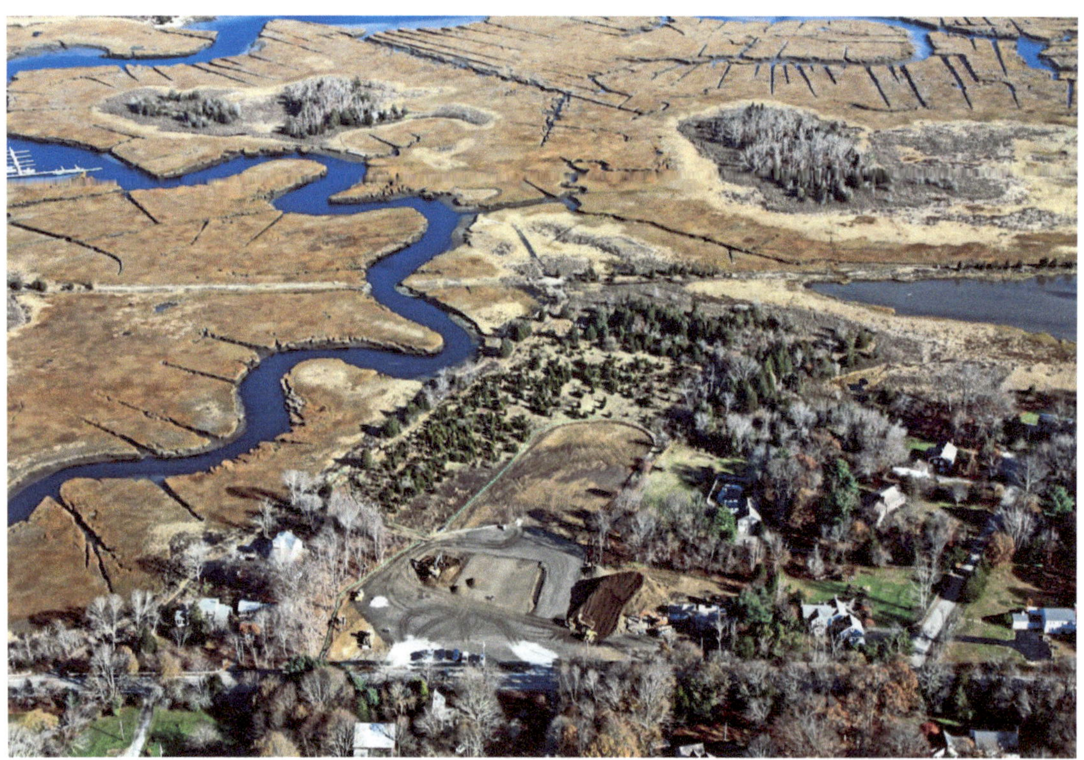

4 From left, Herring River, Wood Island, and Bear Island. Across center is the trail of the Old Colony rail line. Across bottom is Rte 3A, with construction site of four-story, 60-unit affordable housing apartment building, Sanctuary at Herring Brook. [11/21/19]

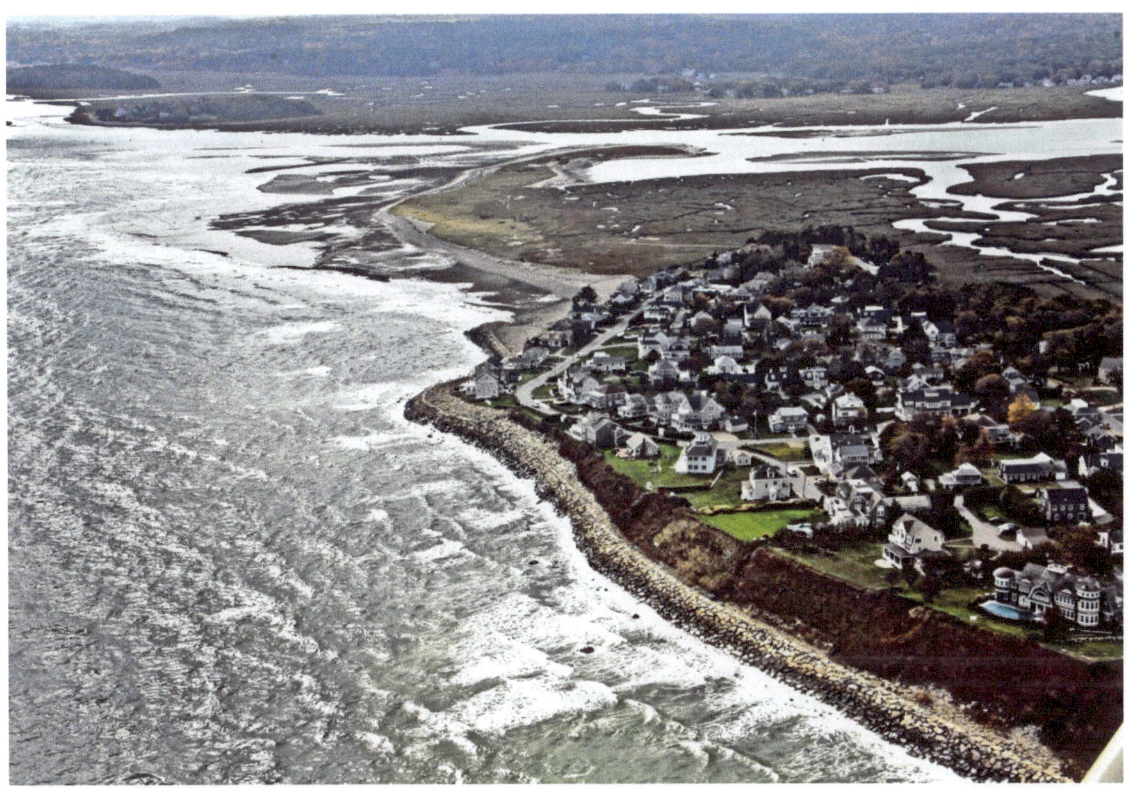

5 View of Rivernoor on Third Cliff, looking south, with the Spit and North River beyond. [10/20/16]

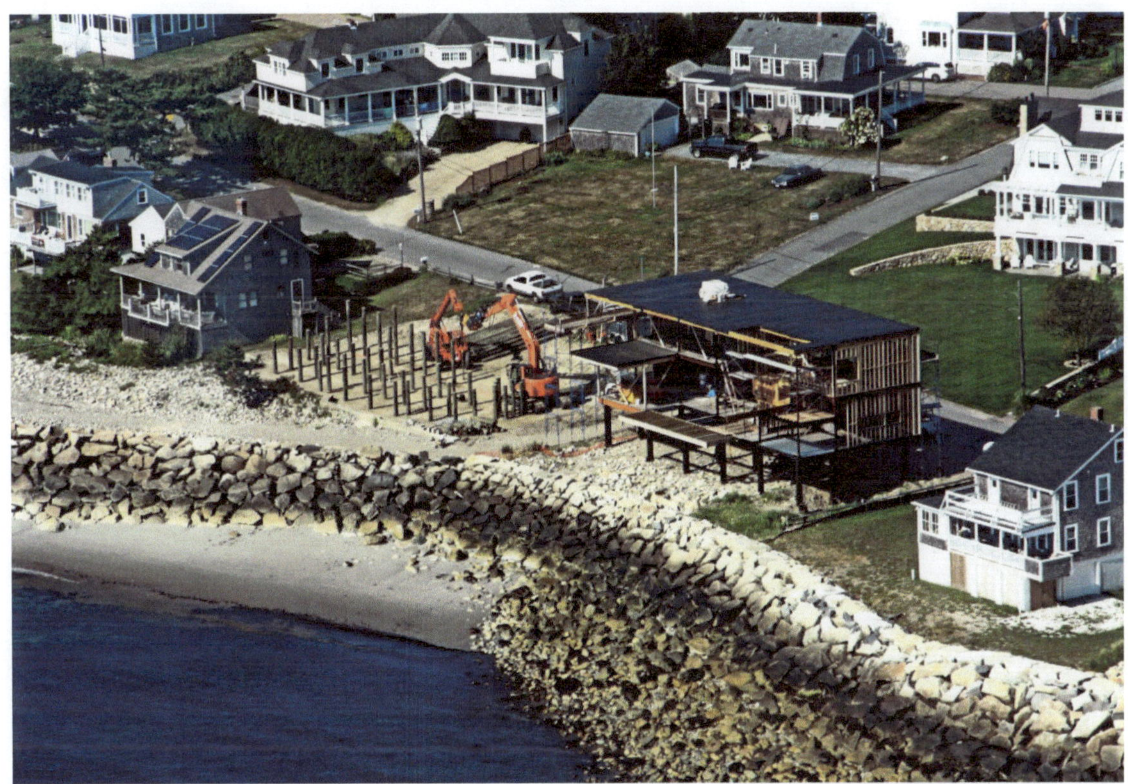

6 Housing construction on pilings at 37 & 43 Collier Rd at Lincoln Ave, behind revetment. [8/29/18]

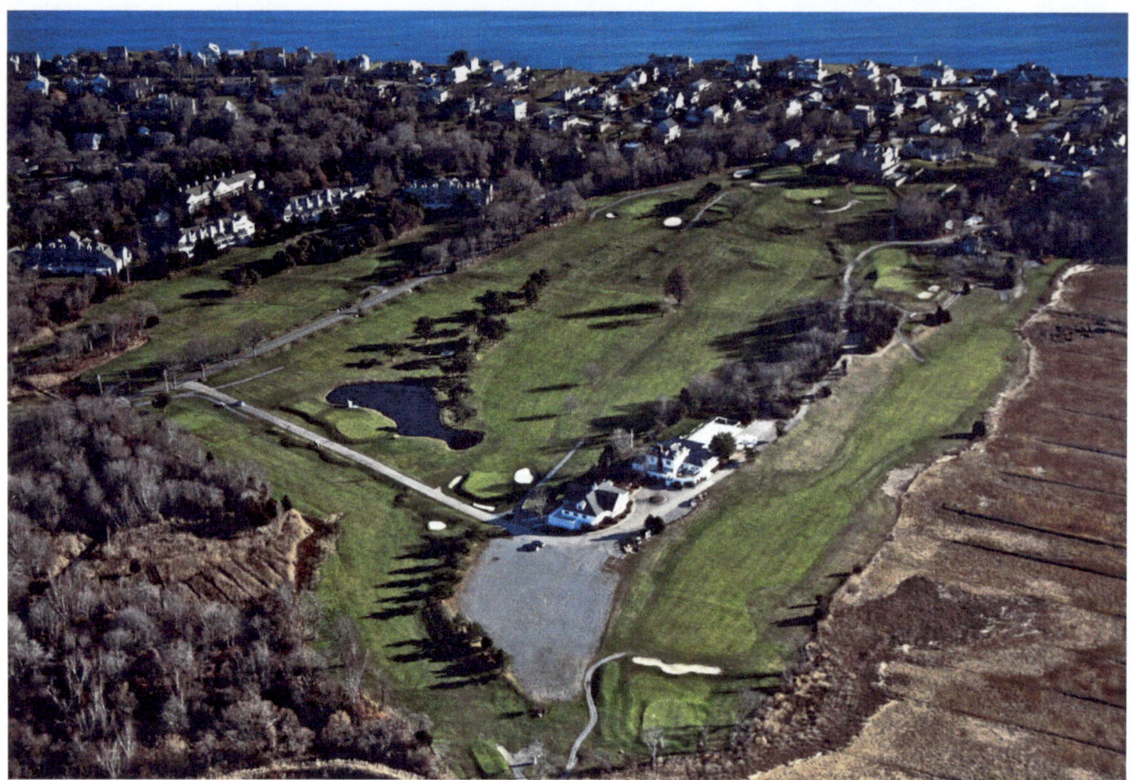

7 Scituate Country Club. Its clubhouse (near center) is an early 1800s farmhouse that was the home for generations of the prominent Welch family. At left, condos at 40 Driftway. At right, North River marshes. [12/4/15]

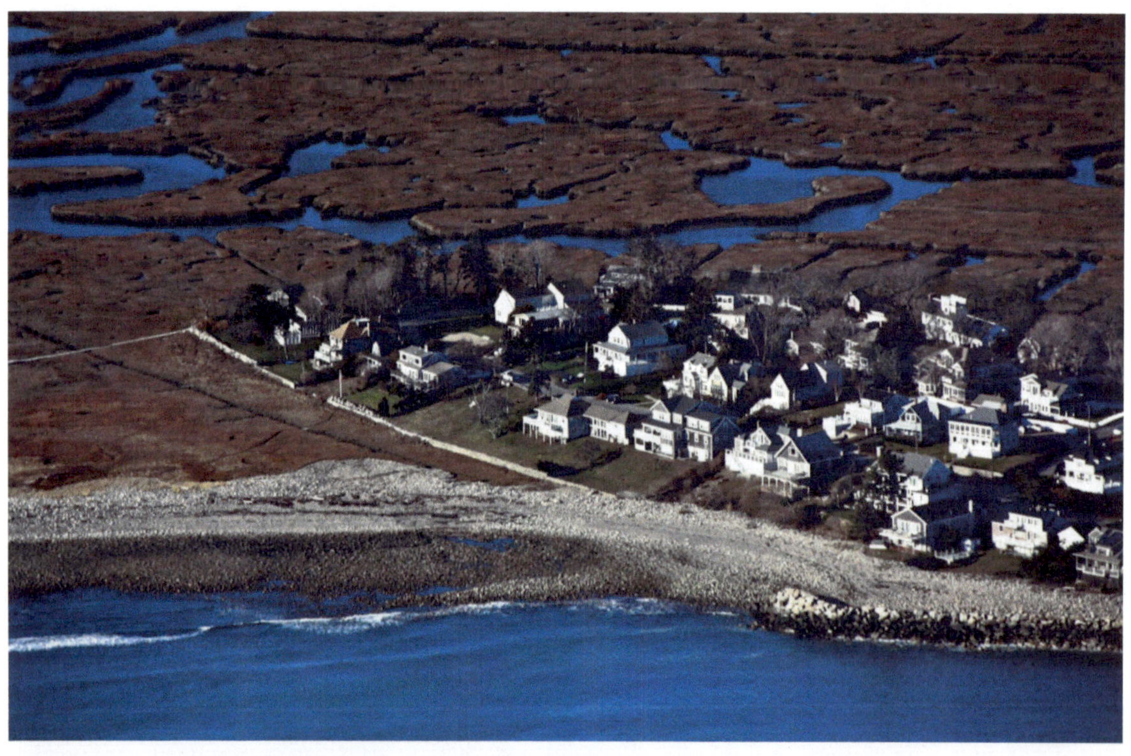

8 Southernmost point of Third Cliff. [12/4/15]

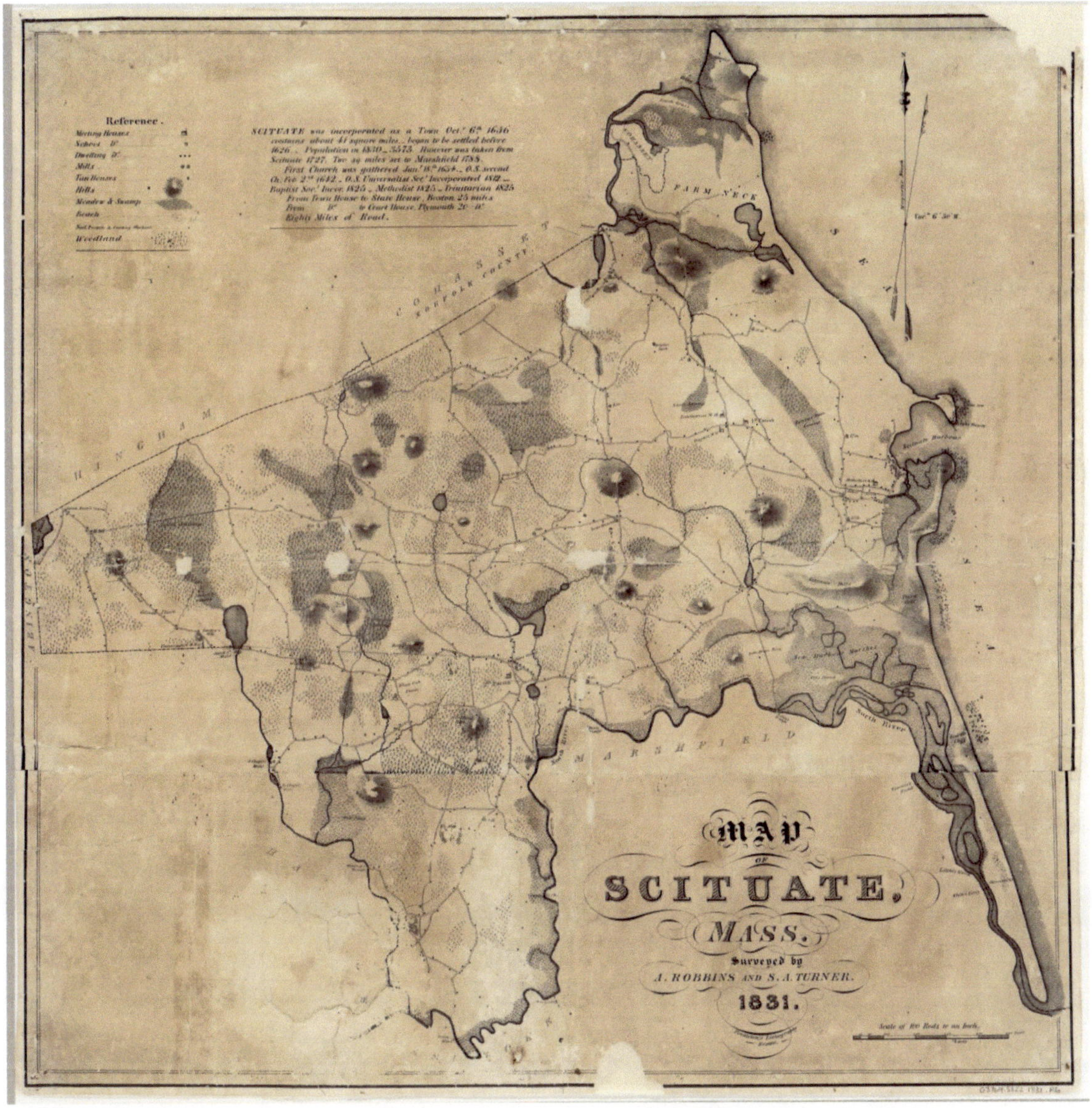

9 *Robbins & Turner 1831 map, showing beach connecting Third Cliff and Fourth Cliff, with "Humarocks" and White's Ferry labeled. Courtesy of Harvard Map Collection.*

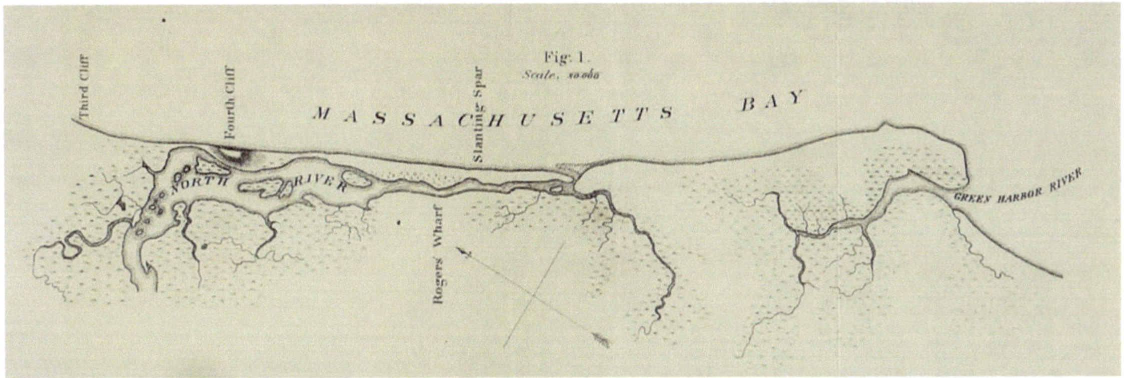

10 *"To accompany report of H. Mitchell on the Reclamation of Tide Lands," detail, 1871 Report of MA Bd. of Harbor Commissioners. Humarock labeled as "Standing Spar." Courtesy of State Library of MA.*

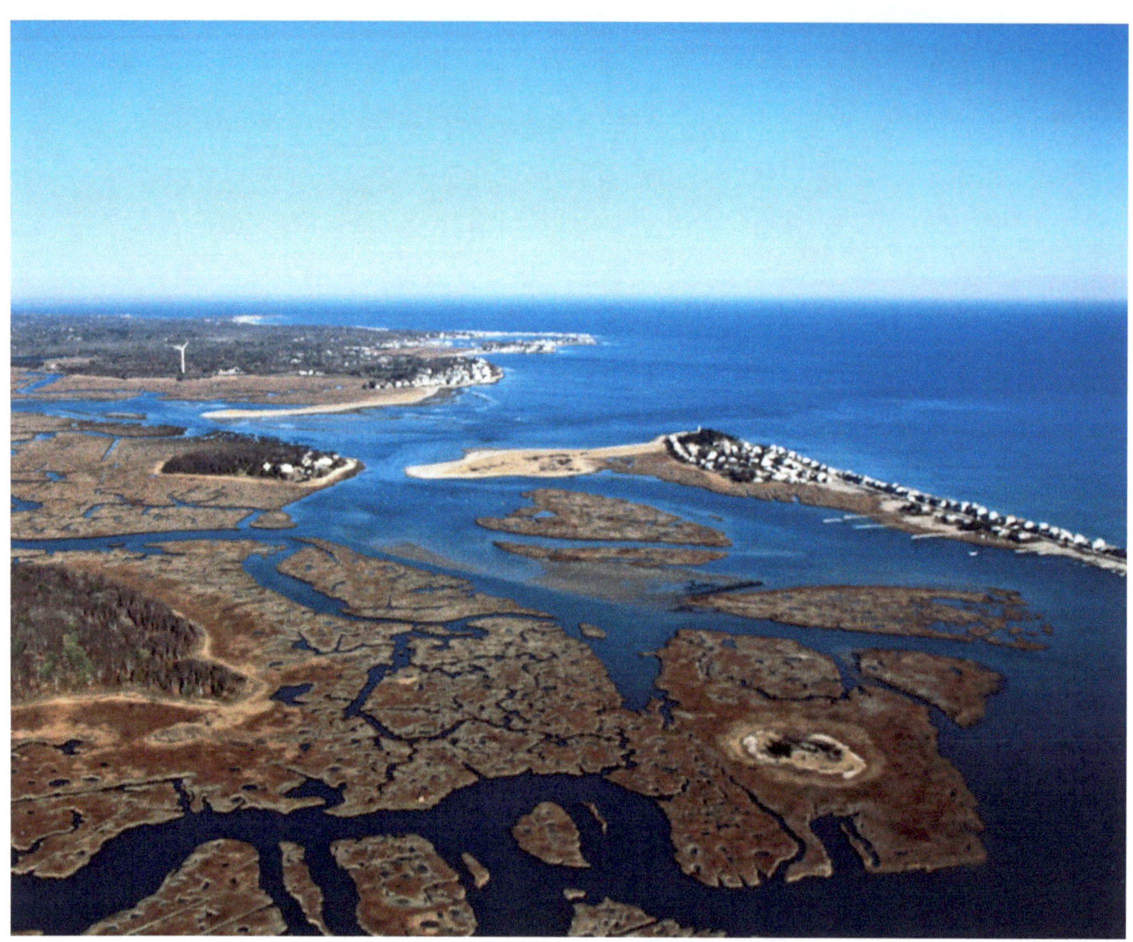

1 From bottom, looking north: South River, Fourth Cliff (light colored beach), North River, other Cliffs, and Scituate Harbor. Beaches at Third Cliff (the Spit) and Fourth Cliff are remnants of beach that connected the cliffs until the Portland Gale of 1898 opened this new mouth of the North River. 12/4/15].

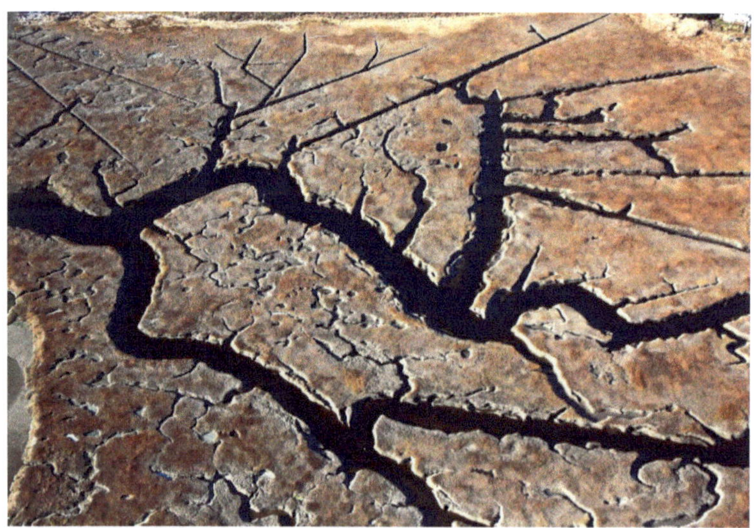

2 Channels and tributaries make complex patterns as they feed the North River and are affected by its tides. [12/4/15]

6

NORTH RIVER, THE SPIT

The North River runs generally west to east, not north. Its name evidently comes from being north of the South River. Both wiggle their way across the landscape until they meet and then exit to Massachusetts Bay. The North River is the only state-protected Scenic River.[18]

The North and South Rivers now meet and exit between Third Cliff and Fourth Cliff, but that was not always the case. Before 1898, these cliffs were connected by a narrow cobblestone beach. As the North River reached that beach, it turned south. It flowed between mainland Marshfield and the narrow Scituate peninsula known as Humarock, until it met the South River and both exited to the sea. That was about three miles south of the cobblestone beach.

The cobblestone beach was breached in the Great Portland Gale of 1898, creating the new mouth of the North River. Remnants of the cobblestone beach turned into a sandy spit of beach at the southern end of Third Cliff, now called "the Spit." The old mouth of the South River closed up.

Today, the Spit at Third Cliff and its counterpart at Fourth Cliff curve up the North River. They are like double gates swung open by ocean tides surging into the mouth of the river. Tides flood the marshes along the river, sometimes turning them into salt water lakes. The marshes, and the river's tributaries, like the Herring River, are ecologically important in sustaining the estuarine food chain and coastal fisheries. The North River, its marshes, and its tributaries are all influenced by the ocean's tides.

The North River was home to centuries of boatbuilding and seafaring, and it still is a home for recreational boating. The North River and its history are explored in a number of books, including L. Vernon Briggs' *History of Shipbuilding on North River,* and John Galluzzo's *The North River: Scenic Waterway of the South Shore.*[19]

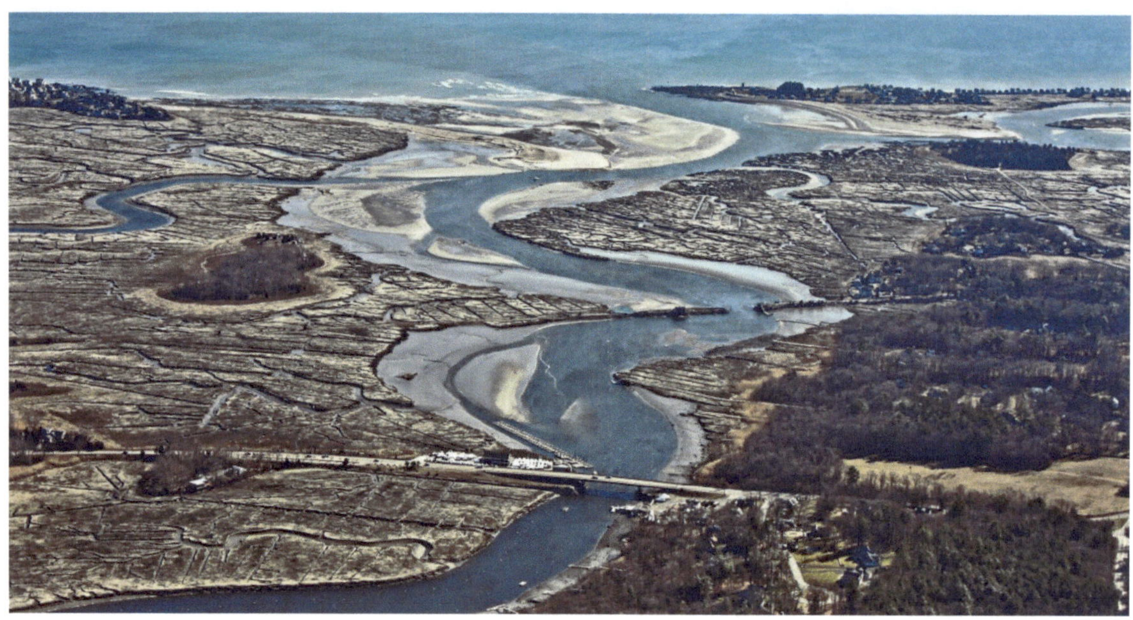

3 The North River meanders to the ocean, between Third Cliff (left) and Fourth Cliff (right). At bottom, Rte. 3A crosses the river. The white rectangular areas just left of the bridge are boats wrapped in plastic for the winter. Above them are remains of a section of the Old Colony railroad line, crossing to Damon's Point in Marshfield. [3/13/20]

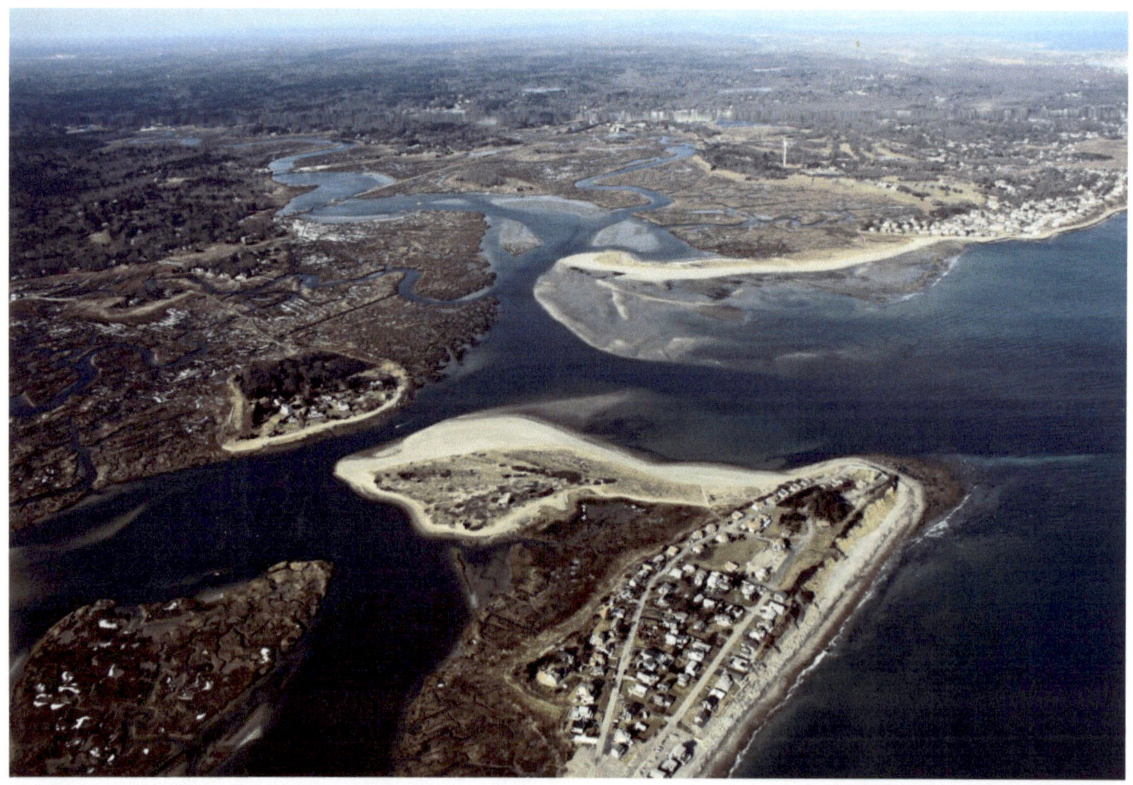

4 Mouth of the North River, looking north. [1/26/18]

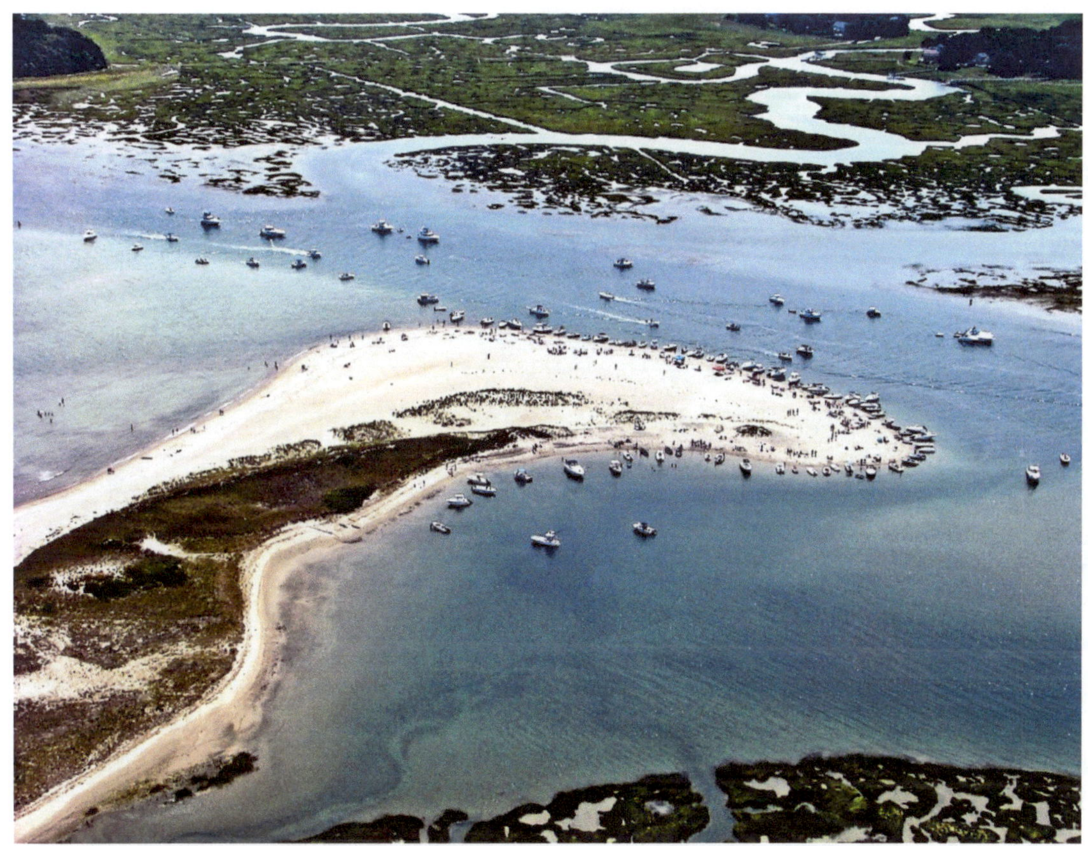

5 The Spit attracts recreational boaters in the summer. [9/3/2005]

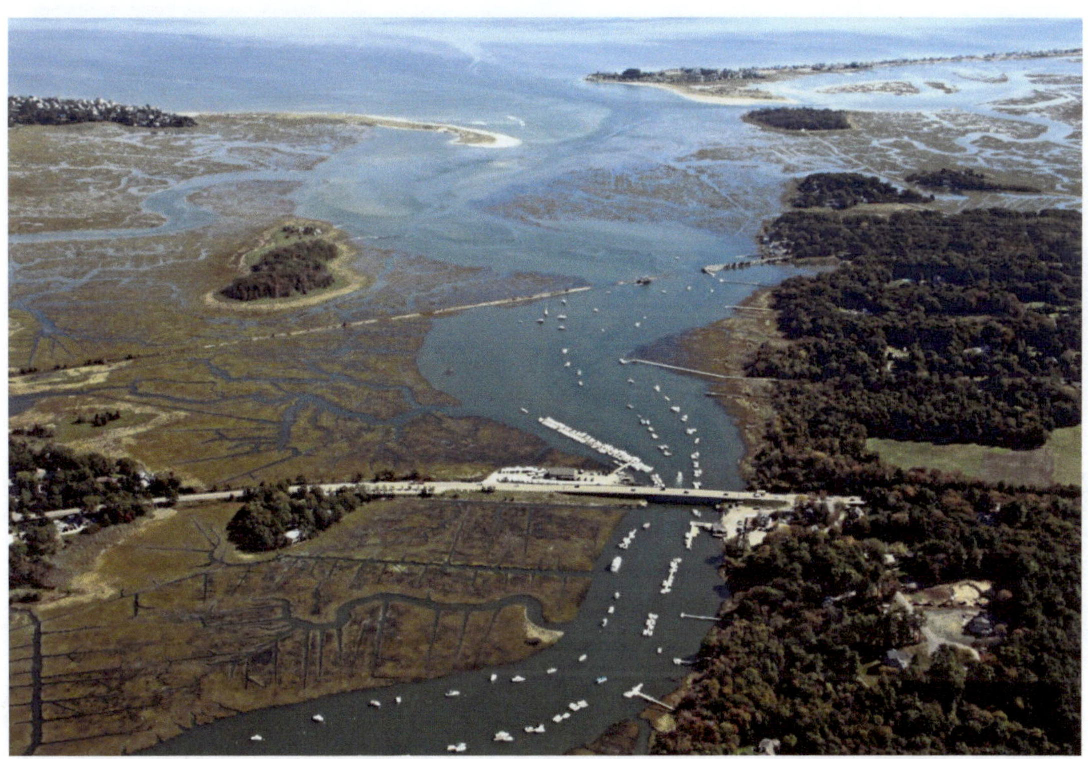

6 North River, looking east, with (from top) Fourth Cliff, the Spit, remains of the Old Colony rail line to Damon's Point, Rte. 3A bridge with Roht Marine marina and lines of moored boats. [10/5/17]

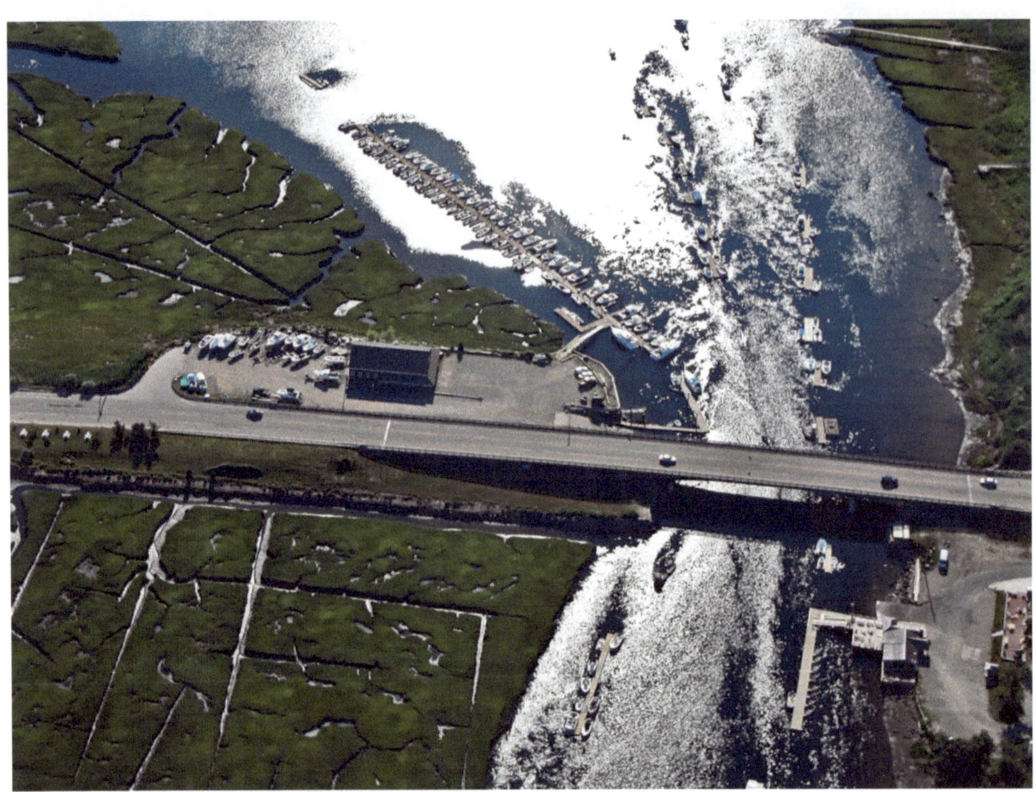

7 Rte. 3A with Roht Marine marina and docked boats. [7/22/15]

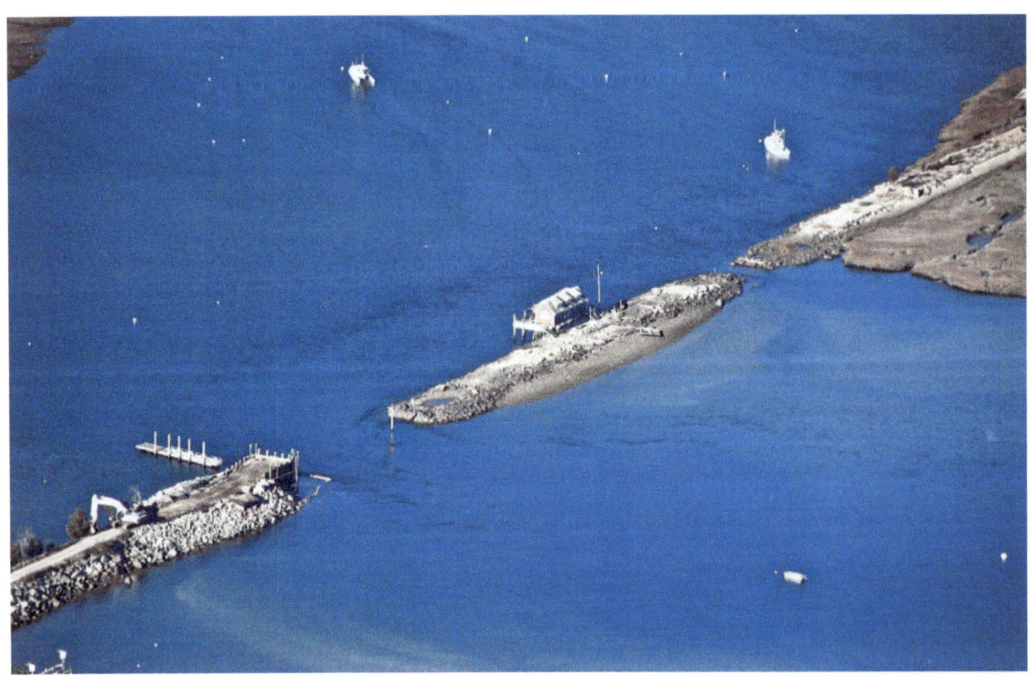

8 At center is the "Dauphtucket" cottage on North River along Old Colony Rail line, possibly the former railroad bridge keeper's cottage. At left is Marshfield town pier at Damon's Point. [12/4/15]

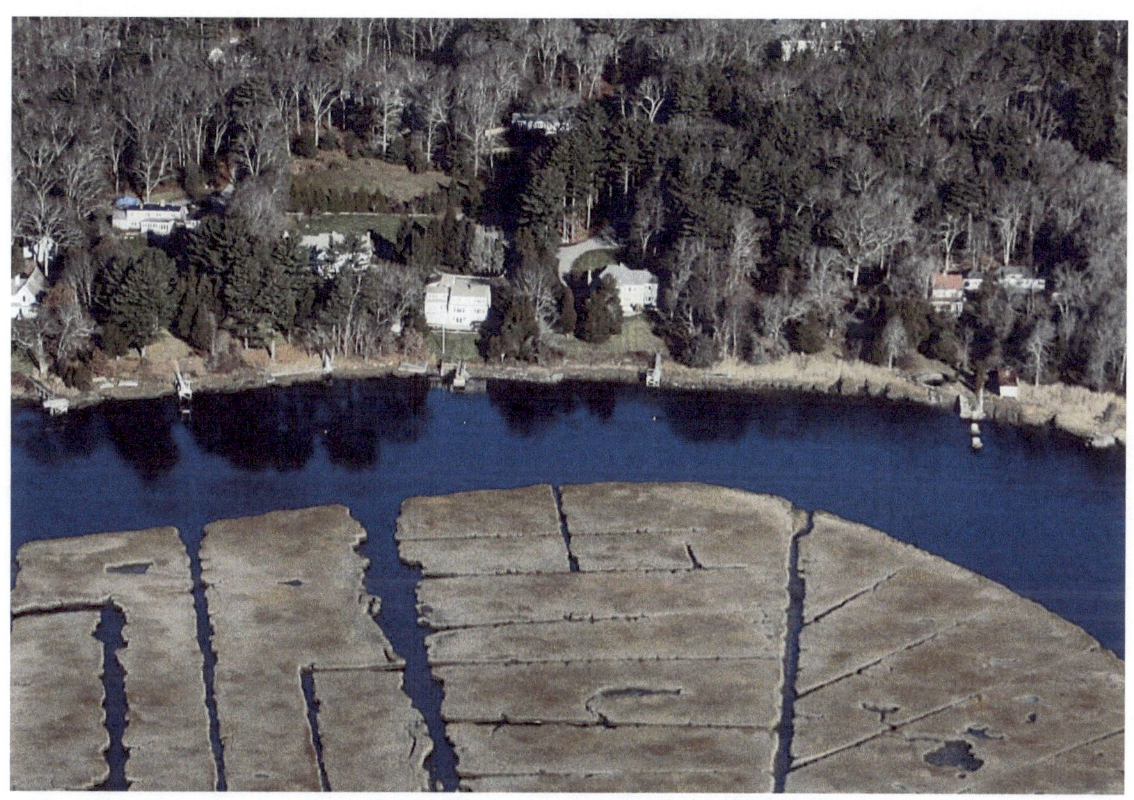

9 Former site of Briggs' Shipyard/Hobart's Landing on the North River. Here ships were built from 1645 to 1842, including the "Columbia" (c. 1773). It was the first American ship to circumnavigate the globe, and it explored (1792) and gave its name to the Pacific Northwest's Columbia River. [12/4/15]

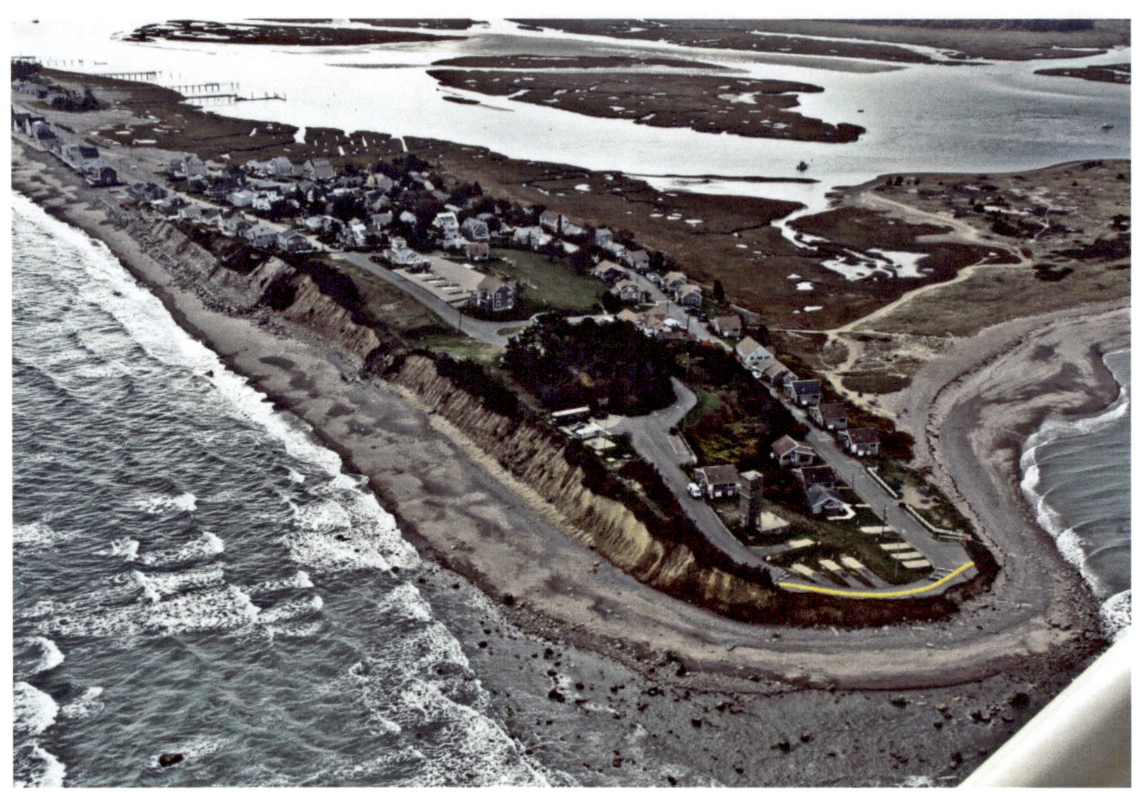

1 North end of Fourth Cliff, ocean on left, South River in background. [10/19/16]

7

FOURTH CLIFF, HUMAROCK, SOUTH RIVER

Fourth Cliff, like the other three cliffs, was named by English settlers soon after their arrival in the early 1630s. There were several large farms on this cliff. It also held one of the first lifesaving stations of the Humane Society of Massachusetts in the 1700s.[20]

The Portland Gale of 1898 isolated Fourth Cliff from the rest of Scituate. That meant that the cliff, and the narrow peninsula (or island) of Humarock on which it is located, can be reached on land only through Marshfield. It became, as it is today, a haven for summer residents.

In the early years of World War II, enemy submarines posed a risk along America's eastern shores. The US built a tower and other facilities at the north end of Fourth Cliff, and similar facilities along the coast, to detect and fire on enemy submarines. The site is now a US Air Force recreation facility with summer cottages.[21]

Humarock has a distinctive history and geography. They are covered in the book by Fred Freitas, *Humarock: Hummocks, Humming Rocks, and Silver Sands*.[22]

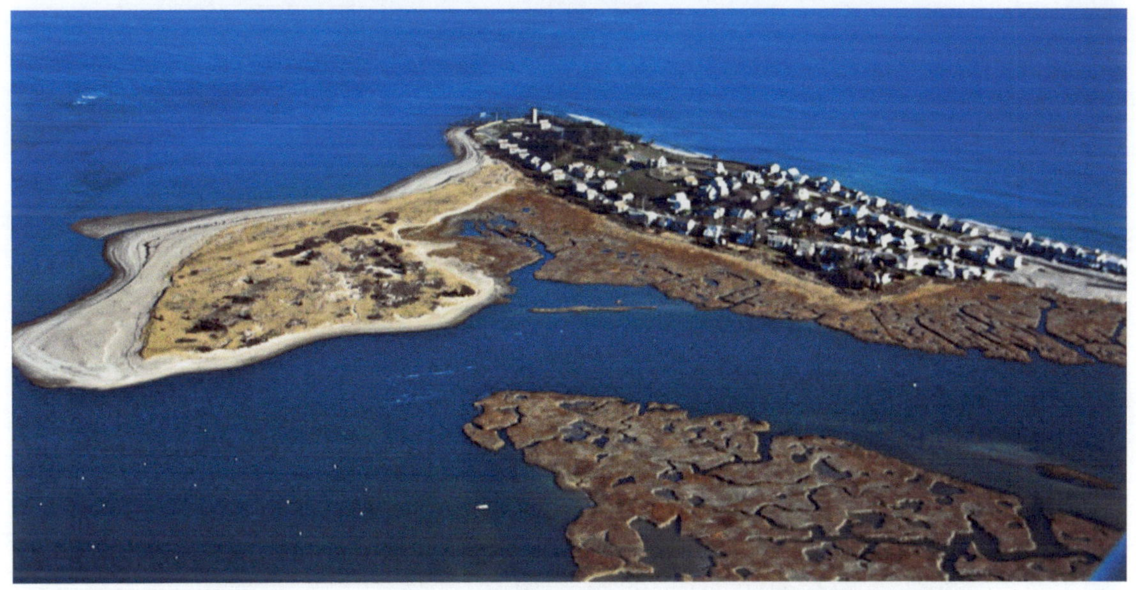

2 Fourth Cliff, view looking east, with South River entering from lower right. [12/4/15]

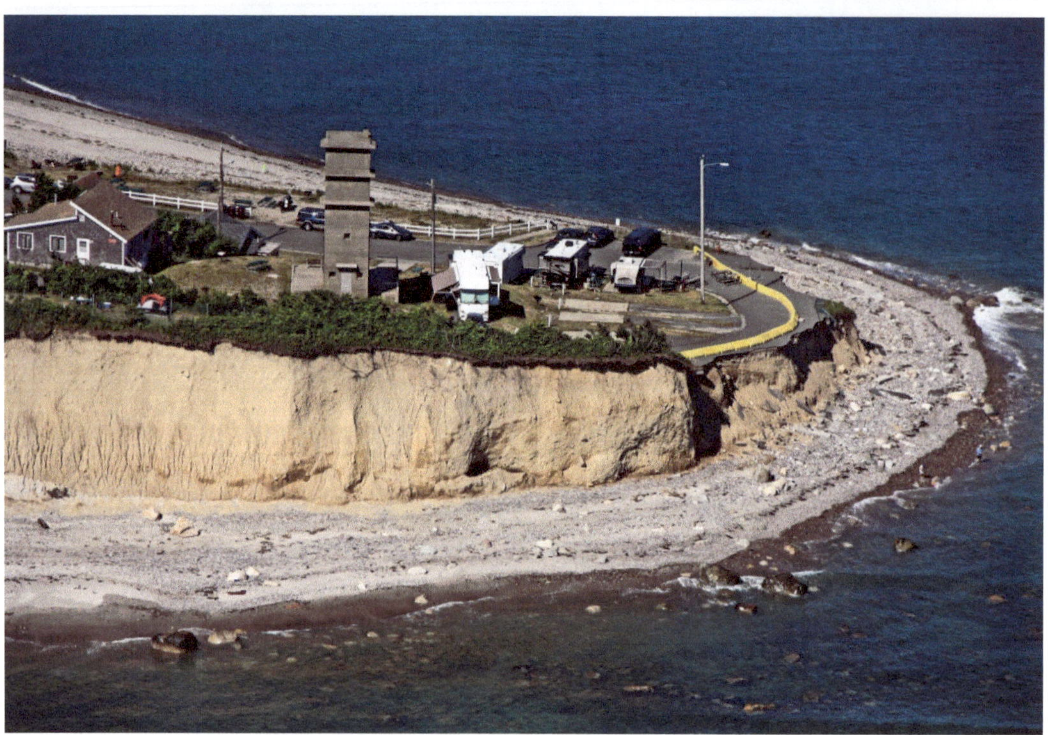

3 At the point of Fourth Cliff is a tower and complex built to sight and fire on enemy submarines during World War II. Now the area is a US Air Force recreational site. [7/15/16]

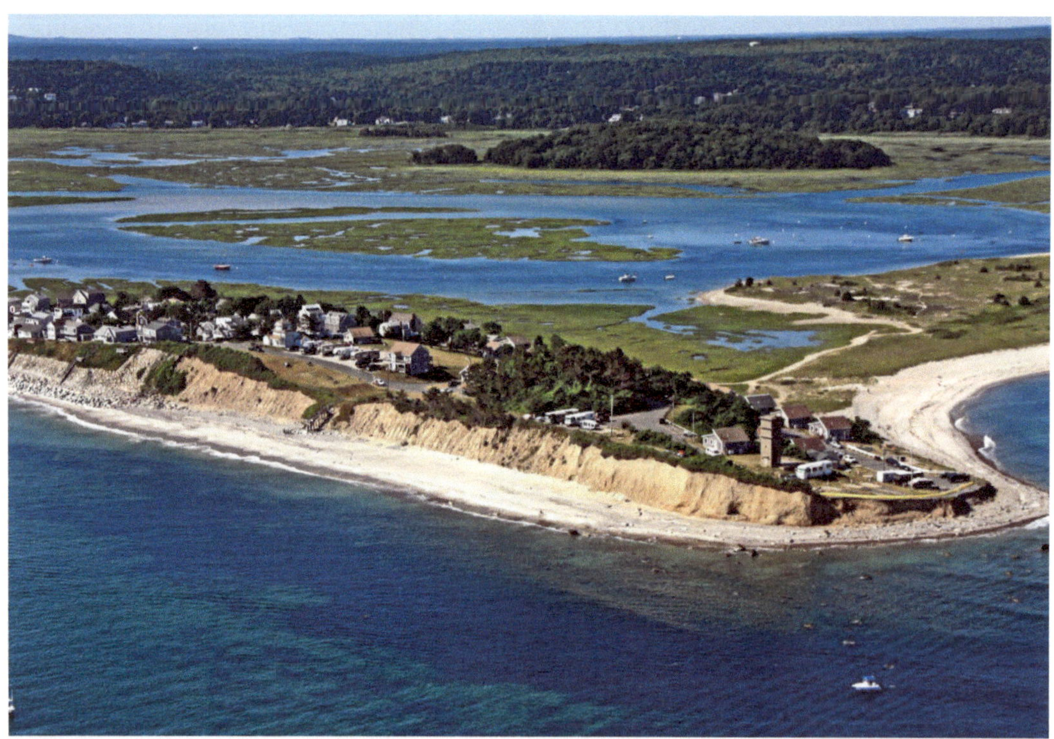

4 It is apparent why this was called a cliff. In the background is the South River and Marshfield, with wooded Tilden Island at upper middle of photo. [7/15/16]

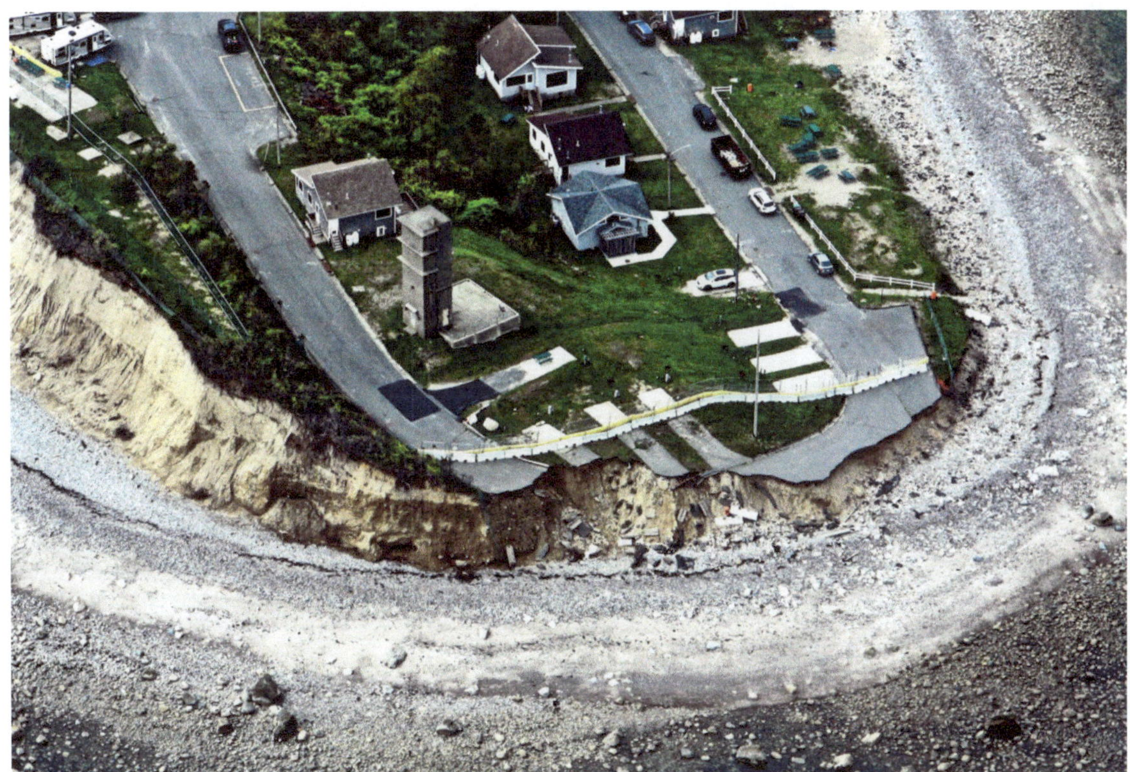

5 The point of Fourth Cliff is crumbling. Compare the placement of the safety barrier here with photos #1 and #3 above. [5/18/19]

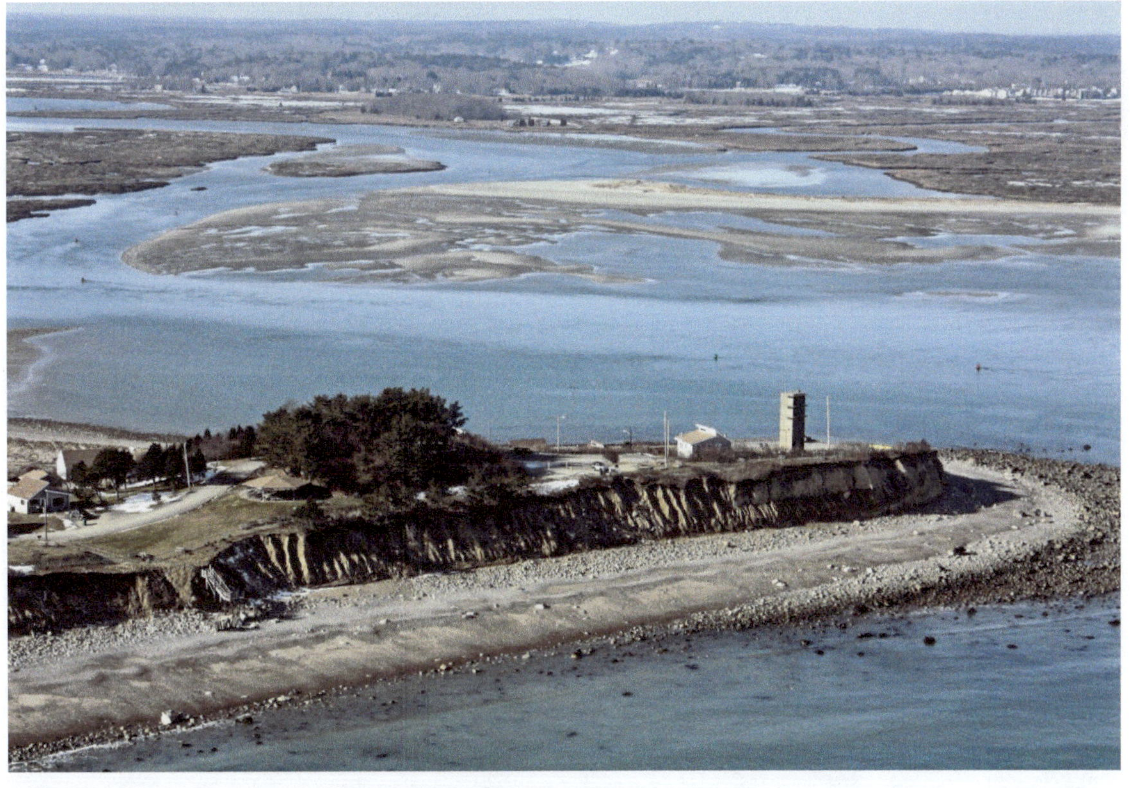

6 Fourth Cliff looking west up the North River. [12/31/10]

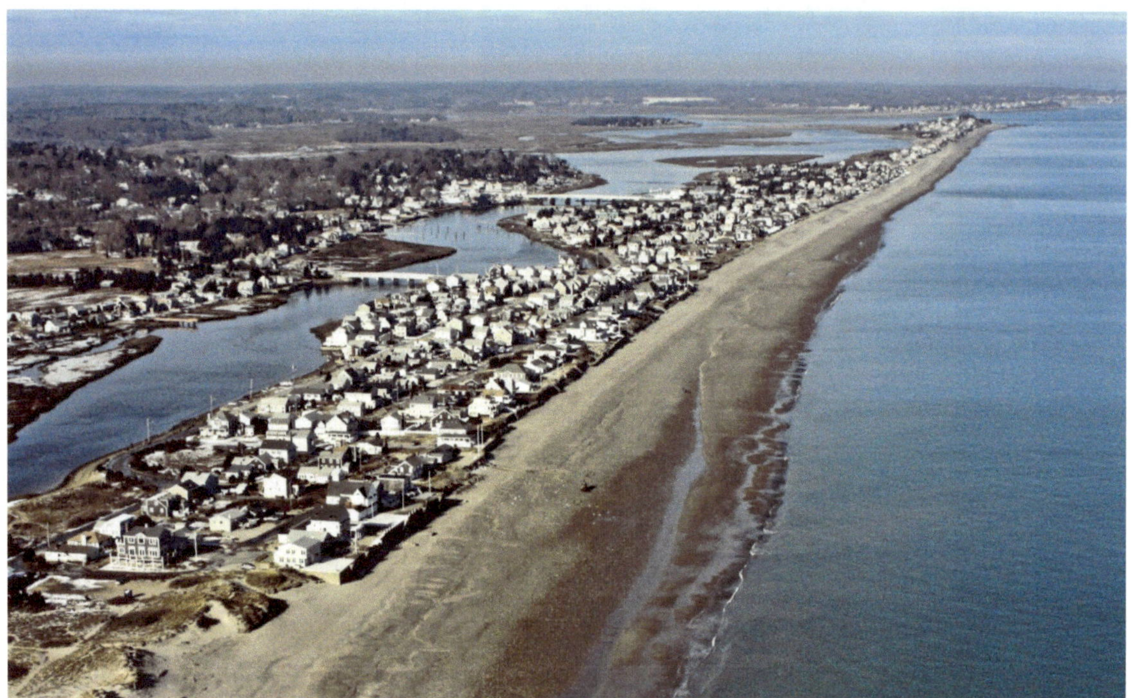

7 Humarock, looking north. The South River is crossed by the Julian Street bridge, and the Sea Street bridge. The Sea Street bridge, rebuilt in 2009, is named for US Lifesaving Service Captain Fred Stanley, who participated in many rescues along Humarock Beach and the Cliffs in the 1800s. [12/31/10]

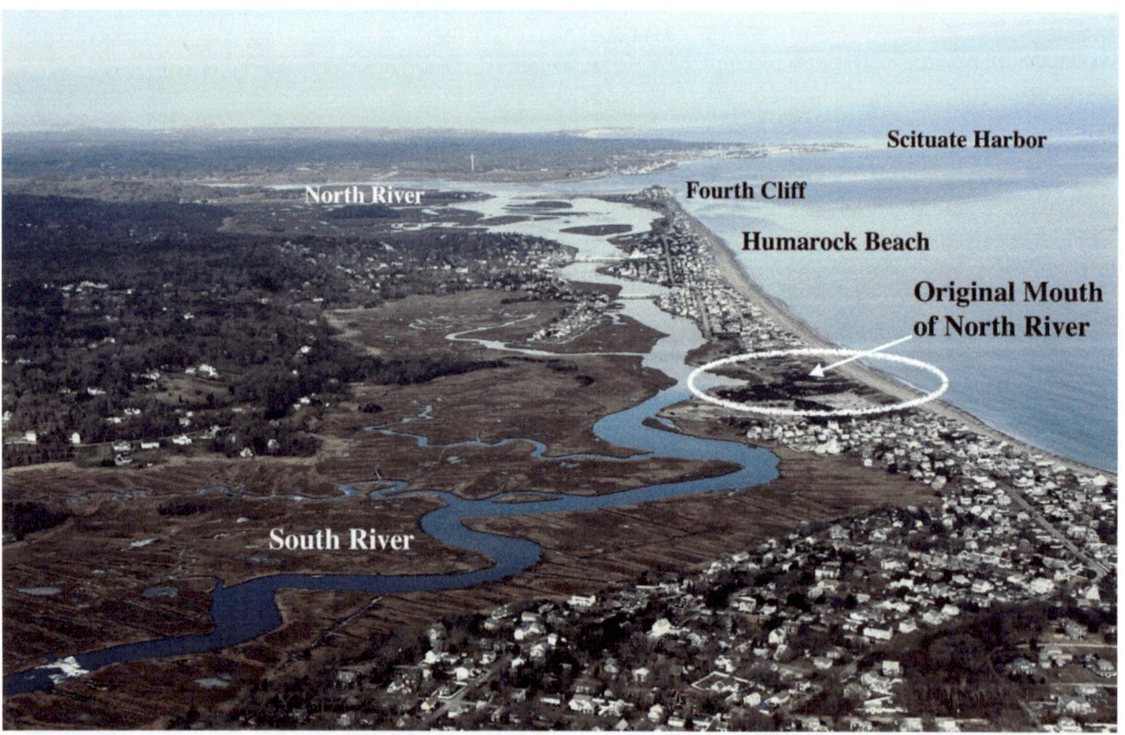

8 View of Humarock and South River looking north. [1/13/22]

NOTES

[1] Wood, William, fl. 1629-1635, Cotes, Thomas, -1641, and Bellamie, John, -1654, "The south part of New England as it planted this yeare, 1634," Boston Public Library, Norman B. Leventhal Map & Education Center, https://collections.leventhalmap.org/search/commonwealth:q524n611v; Joseph F. W. Des Barres, "A Chart of Massachusetts Bay [and Cape Cod Bay]" [1776], in Joseph F. W. Des Barres, *The Atlantic Neptune: The 1802 edition of the Atlantic Neptune, published for the use of the Royal Navy of Great Britain*, Harvard Map Collection, Harvard Library, Cambridge, Mass., Part III: New England to Gulf of Mexico (seq. 41), https://curiosity.lib.harvard.edu/scanned-maps/catalog/44-990020501850203941_FHCL:10188008; Des Barres map for sale at RareMaps.com, https://www.raremaps.com/gallery/detail/59282/massachusetts-bay-with-boston-and-part-of-cape-cod-des-barres; *Town of Scituate*, in J. E. Judson, *Topographical Atlas of Surveys: Plymouth County together with the town of Cohasset, Norfolk County, Massachusetts* (Springfield, MA: L. J. Richards & Co., 1903), plate 31, including insets for Village of Scituate, North Scituate Beach, etc. State Library of Massachusetts, Massachusetts Real Estate Atlas Digitization Project, URI http://hdl.handle.net/2452/206055, http://www.mass.gov/anf/research-and-tech/oversight-agencies/lib/massachusetts-real-estate-atlases.html, and https://www.flickr.com/photos/mastatelibrary/9466953246/in/album-72157634981171273/. Shown elsewhere in this book are (1) the Turner 1795 map, Chas. Turner, *A Plan of the Town of Scituate, in the County of Plymouth, taken in Conformity to Resolve of the General Court, which passed June the 26th 1794*, map, 200 rods to an inch, 1795, Massachusetts State Archives, No. 1242 "Maps and Plans," copy on file, Scituate Historical Society, (2) the Robbins & Turner 1795 map, A. Robbins and S. A. Turner, surveyors, *Map of Scituate, Mass.*, 1 inch = 100 rods (Boston: Pendleton's Lithography, 1831), Harvard Map Collection, Digital Maps, http://vc.lib.harvard.edu/vc/deliver/~maps/MATWN_3764_S322_1831_R6, also on file at Massachusetts State Archives, 1830 series maps, v. 11, p. 2, no. 2095, and (3) detail of map "To accompany report of H. Mitchell on the Reclamation of Tide Lands [probably from Mitchell, H., Appendix No. 1869 - 5. pp. 75-104, US Coastal Survey]," from House document 53 of 1871, 5th Annual Report of the Massachusetts Board of Harbor Commissioners, State Library of Massachusetts, call no. "Map Mass. Marshfield 1870-1," https://state.cwmars.org/eg/opac/record/357798?locg=111, and https://archives.lib.state.ma.us/bitstream/handle/2452/48555/ocm25741276.jpg?sequence=1. In 2021, Scituate resident, author, and illustrator John Roman created a beach towel available for purchase locally that features a map of Scituate; see YouTube video at https://www.youtube.com/watch?v=z48WOhWKt5U.

[2] Colin Schultz, "This Picture of Boston …," April 3, 2013, *Smithsonian Magazine*.

[3] "Cliff Hotel from the air, North Scituate Beach, Mass." Postcard, Tichnor Bros. Inc., Boston, Mass. [ca. 1930–1945], *Digital Commonwealth*, https://ark.digitalcommonwealth.org/ark:/50959/g158br00f; photos in Scituate Historical Society, folder "Scituate Aerial Photos - Harbor, Causeway to Cliffs, Old Oaken Bucket & Point, May 25, 1937."

[4] Garrett Quinn, "Drone Captures Dramatic Flooding at Peggotty Beach in Scituate," *Boston Magazine*, February 12, 2016, https://www.bostonmagazine.com/news/2016/02/12/peggotty-beach-scituate-drone-flooding/; "Winter Storm Riley Batters Scituate, MA," *TIME* Magazine Videos, March 2, 2018, https://www.yahoo.com/news/winter-storm-riley-batters-scituate-210543152.html; "Tracking erosion and coastal storms at Peggoty Beach in Scituate, MA," South Shore Flying Club website, https://www.southshoreflyingclub.com/blog/peggoty-beach-coastal-storm-scituate-ma.

[5] Dates of photos in captions are generally from image/camera metadata, and are not necessarily accurate.

[6] For example, see "Minot's Ledge Light," National Park Service website, https://www.nps.gov/nr/travel/maritime/min.htm; Nancy S. Seasholes, "Minots Ledge Light," NPS website, https://www.nps.gov/boha/learn/historyculture/minots-ledge-light.htm; William Thiesen, "The Long Blue Line," US Coast Guard website, https://www.mycg.uscg.mil/News/Article/2460176/the-long-blue-line-minotsloss-of-the-deadly-lovers-light-170-years-ago/; Patrick Browne, "The Tragic Story of Minot's Ledge Lighthouse," Historical Digression website, https://historicaldigression.com/2015/10/30/the-tragic-story-of-

minots-ledge-lighthouse/; Jeremy D'Entremont, "History of Minots Ledge Light, Scituate, Massachusetts," New England Lighthouses website, http://www.newenglandlighthouses.net/minots-ledge-light-history.html; Dina Fantegrossi, "The Tragic & Creepy History Of Minots Ledge Lighthouse," Chowdaheadz website, https://www.chowdaheadz.com/blogs/news/the-creepy-history-of-minots-ledge-light; Thomas Farragher, "What kind of guy buys a lighthouse? This guy," *Boston Globe*, August 9, 2016, https://www.bostonglobe.com/metro/2016/08/09/what-kind-guy-buys-lighthouse-this-guy/gD60LXII7ON6upvh81mnVL/story.html. It is understood that the light is automated and still operational, with oversight by the US Coast Guard.

[7] Mary B. Hunnewell, *The Glades* (Boston: E. O. Cockayne, private printing, 1914); Bryant F. Tolles, Jr., *Summer by the Seaside: The Architecture of New England Coastal Resort Hotels, 1820-1950* (Hanover, NH: University Press of New England, 2008); "Scituate Open Space and Recreation Plan Update" (Horsely Witten Group, February 9, 2009) Sec. 4.1, p. 24 (350M); Michael Berrill and Deborah Berrill, *Sierra Club Naturalist's Guide to the North Atlantic Coast: Cape Cod to Newfoundland* (San Francisco: Sierra Club Books, 1981), "Geology of the Boreal Coast, Rocks of the Avalon Belt," pages 20-25, Fig. 7, Table 1 (granite ledges formed 350 million years ago)..

[8] "Bassing Beach," Cohasset Conservation Trust website, https://cohassetconservationtrust.org/bassing.html.

[9] John Hartshorne, "*A History of the Gulf River*," May 29, 2002, presentation, available from The Gulf Association, Inc., website; Ruth Thompson, "Scituate voters approve $81.4 million budget," *Patriot Ledger*, June 28, 2020, https://www.patriotledger.com/story/news/local/2020/06/28/scituate-voters-approve-814-million-budget/42558917/.

[10] Pamela L. McCallum & Nancy M. Young, *Memories of The Cliff Hotel* (Scituate, MA: Converpage, 2012).

[11] Barbara Murphy, *Irish Mossers and Scituate Harbour Village* (n.p., 1980); Barbara Murphy, *Scituate: The Coming of Age of a Plymouth Colony Town* (n.p., 1985); David Ball, *To the Point: The Story of Scituate Light and Cedar Point* (n.p.: David Ball, 1994, 6th printing, 2000); Jane K. Thompson, *First Cliff, Scituate, 1630-2013: History of a New England Coastal Neighborhood* (Baltimore, MD: Otter Bay Books, 2013).

[12] Town of Scituate website, https://www.scituatema.gov/community-profile-vision/pages/marine-resources; Bob Mills, "Lobster Fishing Out of Scituate," blog post May 28, 2018, https://www.oatbay00.com/news/2018/5/12/lobster-fishing-out-of-scituate.

[13] Lyle Nyberg, *On a Cliff: A History of Third Cliff in Scituate, Massachusetts* (Scituate: Lyle Nyberg, 2021). The current bridge, the Edward Foster Memorial Bridge, was built in 1930, and dedicated in 1931 with a plaque by local sculptor Cora Overland honoring Scituate veterans of World War I. "Foster, Edward Road Bridge," SCI.901 (1930 bridge), Massachusetts Cultural Resource Information System (MACRIS). The bridge has also been known as the Veterans Memorial Bridge or Edward Foster Bridge (for the road that goes over it).

[14] Lyle Nyberg, *Summer Suffragists: Woman Suffrage Activists in Scituate, Massachusetts* (Scituate: Lyle Nyberg, 2020).

[15] Nyberg, *On a Cliff*, including chapter 3, and sources cited therein.

[16] Nyberg, *On a Cliff*, including 40-41 (the Scituate Country Club, formerly the Welch family farmhouse, was built in the early 1800s).

[17] "Herring Brook Meadow," Stateside Construction Group website, https://stateside1.com/projects/herring-brook-meadow/; Sanctuary at Herring Brook website (with aerial photos), https://sanctuaryatherringbrook.com/.

[18] North River Commission website, http://www.northrivercommission.net/. The NRC has copies of orthomaps of the North River (1978), and other maps, including Commonwealth of Massachusetts, Harbor and Land Commissioner's Office, *Plan of North River in the Towns of Scituate, Marshfield, Norwell, Pembroke & Hanover* (1915), seven sheets.

[19] John Galluzzo, *The North River: Scenic Waterway of the South Shore* (Charleston, SC: The History Press, 2008). See also L. Vernon Briggs, *History of Shipbuilding on North River, Plymouth County, Massachusetts* (Boston: Coburn Brothers, Printers, 1889), https://archive.org/details/historyofshipbui00brigg. The North and South Rivers Watershed Association (NSRWA) has information on its website about Briggs' Shipyard/Hobart's Landing, https://www.nsrwa.org/listing/briggs-yard-hobarts-landing/, Damon's Point, https://www.nsrwa.org/listing/damons-point/, and other features of these rivers.

[20] The Turner 1795 map copied earlier in this book labels this station at the "Hummocks."

[21] Nyberg, *On a Cliff*, ch. 18.

[22] Fred Freitas, *Humarock: Hummocks, Humming Rocks, and Silver Sands* (Scituate: Converpage, 2019).

About the Authors

All three authors live in Scituate and enjoy its beautiful seacoast. Gary and Bill provided an aerial photo for the cover of Lyle's book *On a Cliff*.

Lyle Nyberg, historian and retired lawyer, wrote and published *On a Cliff: A History of Third Cliff in Scituate, Massachusetts* (2021), and *Summer Suffragists: Woman Suffrage Activists in Scituate, Massachusetts* (2020). He can be reached at www.lylenyberg.com.

Gary Banks, former USAF pilot and retired American Airlines Captain, wrote and published *Trysting Pasture and Other Musings* (2013), available at Scituate Historical Society, 43 Cudworth Rd., Scituate, MA 02066.

Bill Richardson, Airport Planner and Site Designer, graduated from the Rhode Island School of Design, and is a former chairman of the Scituate Conservation Commission. He has been flying and taking photos for more than five decades.

We aim for accuracy, but mistakes occur. I, Lyle Nyberg, take responsibility. Let me know and I will try to fix them.